On Eagle's Wings

A Book on Praise and Worship

by

Pastor E. Charlotte Baker

Revival Press

Worship and Praise Division
of
Destiny Image Publishers
P.O. Box 351
Shippensburg, PA 17257

ISBN 1-56043-853-3

For Worldwide Distribution
Printed in the U.S.A.

CONTENTS

DEDICATION
ACKNOWLEDGEMENTS
INTRODUCTION

PART I — THE MESSAGE OF PRAISE

Chapter 1. Introduction to Praise 3
Chapter 2. Praise — A Bible Study 21
Chapter 3. Spiritual Sacrifices 25

PART II — THE MESSAGE OF WORSHIP

Chapter 4. Worship 45
Chapter 5. Bowing in Worship 53
Chapter 6. The Role of Music in the Church ... 83
Chapter 7. "Let them praise His Name in the
            Dance" 99
Chapter 8. God's Principle of Pouring Out 119

BIBLIOGRAPHY

DEDICATION

There are two people in my life to whom I owe so very much, and without whose love and faithfulness this book could never have been written. My beloved husband of 46 years, John, who has never failed to love, encourage, and cover me, and most of all who, in understanding the call of God upon my life, has allowed me to be what I was born to be.

Pastor Reg. Layzell, who through the years faithfully ministered by the Word and counsel to my life on so many occasions. It was Pastor Layzell who pioneered the Message of Praise in the early days of the Latter Rain outpouring and through this my whole life and ministry was revolutionized.

To my husband John (and our two daughters, Juanita and Tammy) and to my faithful pastor, Reg. Layzell, this book is lovingly and gratefully dedicated.

E. Charlotte Baker

ACKNOWLEDGEMENT

There is a special joy and fulfullment which comes to those who write books. This is, I think, reward for the hours of labour and prayer invested. Integrity demands that this be shared with many who make it possible and I am very grateful for all the help I have received along the way.

This is the third printing of *On Eagle's Wings* and remembering all the effort invested in the original printing by the staff and friends at The King's Temple, I say "Thank You"!

Dorothy Natt, whose eagle concept is on the cover, caught something of my spirit and I am grateful.

Evelyn Gallo, my friend, who for many years has lived in our home. She faithfully prayed, interceeded for me and kept the home fires burning so I could be free to write and also pastor and travel.

My sister Julia has unselfishly given of herself, her time and talent to do my office work and help with all details.

I thank John and Rita Hanigan, Carol and Wesley Clark, Shiloh Fellowship, Evelyn Gallo and King's Temple Daycare and many others who have invested their finances to help with the publishing of this book.

INTRODUCTION

In the past few years, much has been written on the subject of praise. This subject is not new, for praise was one of the great truths restored in the 1948 outpouring of the Holy Spirit. Many of God's choice saints of that day invested their all to establish this truth. The message of praise which is now so widely accepted, was in those days rejected and even maligned. This is not to be wondered at, for it is a Bible principle: "Except a corn of wheat fall into the ground and die, it abideth alone: but if it die, it bringeth forth much fruit" (John 12:24). We have seen the message of praise bring forth much fruit.

The words "praise" and "worship" have been used synonymously by many, but further outpourings of the Holy Spirit have brought greater understanding of the terms. In this book we attempt to set forth the message of worship — there is a difference. The reader must always bear in mind that there cannot be an "either/or" concept, for both praise *and* worship are completely essential to the life of the overcoming believer.

There is a very deep cry arising from the hearts of God's hungry people the world over, a cry to "know Him." Worship in its many facets and levels, I believe, is the answer to this cry.

John 4:23 declares, "But the hour cometh, and now is, when the true worshippers shall worship the Father in spirit and in truth: For the Father seeketh such to worship him." The heart-cry of the Father will never be fulfilled until true worshippers are raised up in the Body of Christ.

With these thoughts in mind, and with a deep burden to see God's people enter into new and glorious realms of relationship with Him, this book has been written. To some who read it, it will present a message to be rejected, so be it. To others, as they prayerfully and with open hearts seek out the truth and experience of worship, it will present an open door into His presence.

E. Charlotte Baker

Part One

The Message of Praise

Chapter One

Introduction to Praise

God is in the process of restoring truth to His Church, and among these being restored are "praise" and "worship". The closer we come to the fulness of restoration, and to the fulness of what God is doing in this generation, the more God desires *expression* of praise and worship from His people. Throughout the past years the Spirit of God has shifted activity in praise and worship out of the pulpit into the pew. As we examine history from the dark ages until now, we discover that at the present time there is more congregational participation in worship than there has ever been in the history of the Church. There has never been a time when the sound of praise has been as full and widespread as it is today. We are approaching the last generation which will have the deposit of all truth. Everything God has ever decreed that His people shall know will be deposited into the last-day Church, bringing about the fulness of restoration.

Acts 3:21 tells us that Jesus is restrained in the heavens until the restitution of all things, which God hath spoken by the mouth of all His holy prophets since the world began. Therefore, in order to see what God will do in the last-day Church we must look beyond the book of Acts. We must examine the words of the Old Testament prophets to discover what must be restored to the Church before Jesus returns. The prophets not only provide substantiation for activities of the New Testament Church, but also provide a pattern for the last-day Church, the Church that will experience the fulness of praise and worship, and the fulness of the glory of God.

The seed form of every major Bible truth is presented in Genesis. Each truth is developed throughout the Word of God, reaching its culmination in the book of Revelation. Included with the truths mentioned in Genesis is praise. This chapter will briefly trace the message of praise from Genesis to Revelation, discussing the message of praise as it is being restored to the last-day Church.

Judah

The first mention of praise is found in Genesis 29, the account of the birth of the sons of Leah. Leah and Rachel were wives of Jacob. The Bible tells us that Jacob loved Rachel more than Leah, and when the Lord saw that Leah was hated, He opened her womb. At the birth of her fourth son, Leah said, "Now will I praise the LORD" (v.35). She named this son "Judah." The word Judah means "praise." As we study the Scriptures in which Judah is mentioned, we find that each presents a facet of the message of praise applicable to the Church of The Lord Jesus Christ.

Genesis 49 gives the account of Jacob calling his sons together. The spirit of prophecy came upon him, and he began to prophesy. He said, "Gather yourselves together, that I may tell you that which shall befall you in the last days" (v.1).

Jacob said, "Judah, thou art he whom thy brethren shall praise" (v.8). Jesus sprang out of the tribe of Judah, the only tribe where we see any mention of praise.

"Thy hand shall be in the neck of thine enemies (v.8). True praise is one instrument by which we put our hands on the necks of our enemies. "The hand" in Scripture is a type of ministry.

"Judah is a lion's whelp..." (v.9). Jesus is the Great Lion, the Lion of the tribe of Judah (Rev. 5:5). We are Lion's whelps because we belong to Him.

"The sceptre shall not depart from Judah..." (Gen. 49:10). The sceptre speaks of government. God intended that from the tribe of Judah would come rulership. Spiritual authority accompanies those who know and practice praise. Not every person can cast out devils (Acts 19:14 tells us the seven sons of Sceva tried, but were not successful), but the weakest of God's saints who knows how to praise Him can make a legion of devils run! Spiritual authority comes from the tribe of Judah.

"Until Shiloh come; and unto him shall the gathering of the people be" (v.10). Shiloh refers to Jesus, and it is unto Jesus that the gathering of the people shall be. Praisers are not gathering together around doctrine or unto great men, but unto The Lord Jesus Christ. Jesus is the common denominator of those who praise God. Worshipping, loving, and praising Jesus is what the spiritual tribe of Judah is all about, for Judah is that tribe gathered together unto Him.

God's Dwelling Place

Psalms 22:3 states, "But thou art holy, O thou that inhabitest the praises of Israel." Throughout the ages God has visited many people, but there is only one people with whom He will make His habitation, and that is the people who will praise Him. God is saying, "I am holy, but I will have a dwelling place on earth. The place which I will inhabit is where My saints are praising Me."

"Blessed is the people that know the joyful sound: they shall walk, O LORD, in the light of thy countenance. In thy name shall they rejoice all the day: and in thy righteousness shall they be exalted" (Ps. 89:15,16). Some people feel that praise is meaningless noise; others, in tune with heaven, identify praise as a joyful sound which pleases the heart of God. God says the people to whom praise is a joyful sound are blessed, and shall walk in the light of His countenance. The ability to walk in the light of God's countenance is given to us when we learn and practice praise.

The terrified enemies of Israel said of God's people "The shout of a king is among them" (Num. 23:21). The enemies did not understand the sound of praise, but they identified it as the shout of a King. They knew that Israel could not be defeated, for within Israel was an ability to touch God. Today, as spiritual Israel, we can sing, "Rejoice not against me, O mine enemy:" (Mic. 7:8), because the shout of the King is among us.

A Sign of Blessing

During the grape harvest, the people who gathered in the vineyards would sing one to another of the goodness of God and of the ingathering of the plentiful harvest. The workers would pour baskets of grapes into a vat, and the barefooted women would go inside the vats and tread out the grapes, and as the new wine was flowing, they would sing and shout across the vineyard to one another of the goodness of the Lord and of the joy of harvest. When God brought judgment upon Israel, crops were devastated and there was no joy at the time of harvest. God said that a sign of His judgment upon a people would be that vineyards would be silent, and the vintage shouting would cease (Isa. 16:9,10). When we are out of the will of God, our vintage shouting ceases. Instead of calling to the person in the vat next to us and saying, "How is it going for you? The Lord is good," we begin to hang our heads. The silencing of praise indicates the hand of God's blessing has been lifted.

Psalms 137 tells us that when the children of Israel were in bondage, they had no song. The voice of praise was stilled in their midst. In verses 3 and 4 they asked of those who had wasted them, "How shall we sing the LORD'S song in a strange land?" When we enter a strange land or when we travel beyond the perimeter of the Kingdom of God, the songs of Zion do not sound so good. When we are in a strange land, we might as well hang our harps upon a willow tree, for we have no joy. When we enter into the Kingdom of God and when we are walking in His will, we can sing the song of the Lord, we can be filled with joy because bondage and barrenness have been removed from our lives, and upon our lives has been placed the blessing of God.

Gates of Praise

The Bible refers to praise as a gate. Isaiah 60:18 states, "Thou shalt call thy walls Salvation, and thy gates Praise." The purpose of a gate is to provide a place of entering. Praise is an entering into the presence of God. At the first veil of the tabernacle we stand in the "bless me" realm, where we praise God if He blesses us; but at the altar of incense we stand as kings and priests who come before the Lord not to be blessed but to bless Him. We walk through the gates of praise into the precious experience of ministering unto the Lord.

The walls of salvation form the perimeter of praise. If a man has not been born again, he should not be expected to praise God, for to the *unsaved* man, praising the Lord is folly and nonsense. As soon as a man has been born again, he should be taught the message of praise. We should not say to the newborn Christian, "As a babe in Christ, I don't think you should praise the Lord or do any of those deep spiritual things until you are more mature." After the babe has taken his first breath in the Kingdom, he should be taught to praise the Lord. When he comes through the gates of praise, he will not only enter into the presence of God, but he also will begin to know and to experience the truths of God's Kingdom.

Isaiah 62:10 instructs people to go *through* the gates. There are many people who have approached the gates, have seen the word, "praise," and have said, "Hallelujah! I will build a tabernacle right here." These people have built a tabernacle upon one truth. However, the message of praise is a progressive, ever enlarging message, through which we walk in order to get somewhere else. The Word instructs us to go through the gates, to cast up the highway, to gather out the stones (or the stumbling blocks), and to lift up a standard for the people. Until we have moved through the gates of praise, we cannot do these other things. Sometimes a person comes to church feeling tired. He has been working all week, and says to himself, "I just don't feel like praising the Lord." However, those in the congregation who know the message of praise *will* praise the Lord. Stumbling blocks of tiredness, worry and even illness are cast out of the way when a congregation learns to praise the Lord.

When there is an engagement in spiritual warfare, the atmosphere often becomes difficult. At such times we make war with the weapon of praise that God has given to His people. When bringing a person through deliverance who is depressed, troubled, harassed by the enemy; it is essential to go through the 'gates of praise' so the atmosphere can be charged with the presence of God. "I will praise Thee: for Thou hast heard me, and art become my salvation" (Ps. 118:21).

Praise is not something we experience occasionally, but is a garment which will be worn constantly by the last-day Church (Isa. 61:1-3). The garment of praise is the perfect answer for the depressions which are common to this generation. No nervous condition or depression can stand in the presence of one who wears the garment of praise. When we praise the Lord in the midst of depression, the atmosphere in which God loves to dwell is created, the spirit of heaviness lifts and we are clothed with praise. There is no excuse for depression in God's people. Until we have learned to control the "black cloud," we cannot enter into the fulness of worship.

Another reason we enter the gates of praise is revealed in Psalms 49:4: "I will incline mine ear to a parable: I will open my dark saying upon the harp." When the prophetic anointing came upon David, he often uttered "dark sayings," things which he, himself, did not understand. As David played his harp, sang, and praised God, the dark sayings were opened. Just as the Word of God was opened to David through praise, so today the Scriptures are opened to God's people through praise. When we find portions of the Word of God difficult to understand, we should begin to sing and to praise the Lord. There is a place in the presence of God where He will shed His light upon the "dark sayings," opening His Word unto His people.

Righteousness and Praise are United

Isaiah 61:10 and 11 declares, "I will greatly rejoice in the LORD, my soul shall be joyful in my God; for he hath clothed me with the garments of salvation, he hath covered me with the robe of righteousness, as a bridegroom decketh himself with ornaments, and as a bride adorneth herself with her jewels. For as the earth bringeth forth her bud, and as the garden causeth the things that are sown in it to spring forth; so the LORD GOD will cause righteousness and praise to spring forth before all the nations." Which of you is responsible for walking up and down in the city and causing the crocus buds to burst forth, the daffodils to bloom, and the trees to burst into blossom? Which of you is responsible for the beauty of springtime? You could go outside on a rainy winter's day and say, "Spring up, O ye daffodils. Spring up, O crocuses. Blossom, O ye trees," and people would call you insane! At the *appointed time*, the earth springs forth with new life. It is God's sovereign time for the earth to bring forth that which has been deposited in it. No amount of rebuke could change that timing, and no command of man can change the life that is springing forth. In the same way, from all the earth the Kingdom of God will spring forth before all nations. In the last days, all nations will see and hear the message of righteousness and praise. True praise springs forth from a righteous life. When we praise the Lord and worship Him we are changed into His likeness. A righteous people who praise the Lord, will bring the knowledge of the glory of the Lord into all the earth!

The Generation of Praise

We cannot deny that we are living in the last days. Every prophetic Word that has not yet been fulfilled can be fulfilled rapidly, and we cannot count on the Church having much more time. When we read Scripture which states, "in that day" such as, (Isa. 2:1-11, 17, 20; Isa. 52:6; Matt. 7:22) we cannot count on that day being too far away. That day is upon us! We must take a good look at what the Bible is saying, and then look at the world today. Many events which follow the statement "in that day" have already come to pass; others are presently being fulfilled. This is consistently true throughout the Word of God.

Psalms 102:16 states, "When the LORD shall build up Zion, he shall appear in his glory." Who can deny that in this day God has built up the Church? At the time I was saved, a person who received the Baptism of the Holy Spirit would have landed outside the doors of my denomination in great fashion! Today the Holy Spirit has invaded every denomination. Every place where God's people are fulfilling His Word and are walking by principle, God is building up Zion. Instead of saying that this prophetic Word will be fulfilled in the millennium or at some future time, we should take a good look at the Church, for God is building Zion today. Malachi 3:1 declares, "The LORD, whom ye seek, shall *suddenly* come into his temple," for God is appearing in the glory which He is putting upon His Church. The Lord shall suddenly appear in His temple, in the midst of a people who will praise His Name.

"He will regard the prayer of the destitute and not despise their prayer" (Ps. 102:17). God always meets a people who are destitute; who know they have nothing. Such people cry out to God, "While you are building the Church, please include me in everything You are doing." The Lord will not despise their prayer.

"This shall be written for *the generation* to come" (Ps. 102:18). There is one generation to come to whom these Scriptures apply. The Bible tells us that the generation which will be created in the last days shall praise the Lord. Praise will be the earmark of the generation which will bring about the breaking of the appointment with death. Praise will no longer be offered to God on a "bless me" basis, but will be given as spiritual kings and priests come before the altars of their God, offering sacrifices unto Him.

Today God has invaded every denomination. He is creating a spiritual generation which will praise Him. If you want to receive a blessing, go to a country in which the people speak a language other than your own. Worship with that people, and listen as they praise the Lord. As you praise the Lord in your own language, and mingle your praise with their praise, you will receive a special blessing as you experience the literal fulfillment of Isaiah 61:11, "For as the earth bringeth forth her bud, and as the garden causeth the things that are sown in it to spring forth; so the Lord GOD will cause righteousness and praise to spring forth before all the nations." Today we are living in the generation of those who will see the culmination of all things. We are living in *the generation* created to praise the Lord!

Restoration

God is moving quickly to bring to pass in the Church all things which He has spoken from the mouth of His holy prophets. In the last-day Church will be a restoration of praise and worship. There is a definite spirit of praise among people who are enjoying the blessing of restoration.

"And they shall come from the cities of Judah, and from the places about Jerusalem, and from the land of Benjamin, and from the plain, and from the mountains, and from the south, bringing burnt offerings, and sacrifices, and meat offerings, and incense, and bringing sacrifices of praise, unto the house of the LORD" (Jer. 17:26). Jeremiah saw a stream of people from the nations of the earth bringing sacrifices into the house of the Lord. He saw a Church which would be the fulfillment of the burnt offerings and the meat offerings. Because the natural sacrifices were fulfilled in Jesus, the sacrifice of praise is something only New Testament priests may offer. Jeremiah is literally saying there will be a tremendous ingathering in the last-day Church. People will come from everywhere, bringing spiritual sacrifices and the sacrifice of praise into the house of the Lord.

Jeremiah 30:19 declares that with the restoration of praise will be the restoring of voices of thanksgiving and joy. Verses 20 and 21 promise that not only will God establish the congregation of the last-day Church in His presence, "their congregation shall be established *before me*" (v.20), but also that He will multiply the congregation. God promises to train the ministries of the last-day Church in the midst of the congregation. "And many people shall go and say, Come ye, and let us go up to the mountain of the Lord, to the house of the God of Jacob; and He will teach us of His ways, and we will walk in His paths: for out of Zion shall go forth the law, and the word of the Lord from Jerusalem. (Is. 2:3) He has also purposed that His people would multiply themselves and be governed by God appointed, spirit anointed ministries, and trained in the house of the Lord.

God is demanding of the ministry today a higher standard than ever before. He is dealing with us, convicting us and making us know that the ministry must be pure. Woe be unto the ministries who walk in unrighteousness or allow unrighteousness in this last day! If God caused us to walk in holiness in the early days of this outpouring when the message of praise was birthed, then in this day when we are about to see God sweep suddenly into His temple, may the Lord help us who believe and teach the message of praise to walk a holy walk!

Today the Spirit of God is sweeping through His Church. Waves of repentance are coming, causing His people to be cleansed. As God refines and purifies His people, He also purifies the "sons of Levi" — the ministry. Malachi 3:3 tells us that when the sons of Levi are purged by fire as silver and as gold, they will offer unto the Lord an offering in righteousness. When they present this offering in righteousness, the offering of Judah will be pleasant unto the Lord.

The Restoration of Joy and Gladness

The restoration of joy and gladness is again mentioned in Jeremiah 33:10 and 11. This passage was written when Israel was still offering blood sacrifices. Jeremiah received revelation of a day beyond his time, when the Church would be desolate, ravished, and in trouble. In this revelation, he saw the glory of God restored to the Church. He saw the restoration of the power and the anointing of the Holy Spirit. He heard the Lord say, "In this place where people say there will be no more glory or power, I will restore some voices." God revealed to Jeremiah a Church which would be filled with, "the voice of joy, the voice of gladness, the voice of the bridegroom (prophecy), and the voice of the bride (the Church responding to the prophetic voice), the voice of them that say, Praise the LORD of hosts: for the LORD is good; for his mercy endureth for ever."

These are signs of the last-day Church that is walking in the fullness of restoration. They will bring neither a turtledove, a lamb, nor an heifer (Heb. 13:11) but will bring a greater sacrifice than these, for they will bring the sacrifice of praise into the house of the LORD. Just as Israel came to the house of the Lord with sacrificial animals, so we, as kings and priests, come unto the house of the Lord with our mouths full of praise, offering to God the sacrifices which are pleasing unto Him.

Zacharias

When Zacharias was told that he and Elisabeth would have a son, he did not believe it. Gabriel, an angel sent by God to Zacharias, said, "And behold, thou shalt be dumb, and not able to speak, until the day that these things shall be performed, because thou believest not my words, which shall be fulfilled in their season" (Luke 1:19,20). In due time, Elisabeth conceived, and bore a son. Zacharias communicated this information, his mouth was opened immediately and his tongue loosed; he spoke and praised God. Zacharias had been set free! His first words were praise. There are times in our lives when we refuse to believe the Word of the Lord because its fulfillment seems impossible in the light of our natural circumstances. At those times God will often "shut our mouths" so that we will not speak words of unbelief. When we finally see the Word of the Lord come to pass, our tongues are loosed that we might praise the Lord, giving God glory for the fulfillment of His Word.

The Birth of Jesus

Another example of praise is given in Luke 2:13 and 14. The Bible tells us that heaven and earth glorified God at the birth of Jesus. Indeed all heaven joined in one great anthem of praise unto God: "Glory to God in the highest, and on earth peace, good will toward men." As the shepherds beheld the Babe, they also glorified God, praising Him for all the things they had heard and seen (Luke 2:20).

Jesus' Triumphal Entry into Jerusalem

Jesus' triumphal entry into Jerusalem was so filled with praise that all the city was moved, saying, "Who is this?" The multitude answered, "This is Jesus the prophet of Nazareth of Galilee" (Matt. 21:10,11). When Jesus entered the temple the children followed Him, praising God and saying, "Hosanna to the Son of David" (v.15). The Chief Priests and Scribes were displeased. Jesus silenced their criticism, saying, "Have ye never read, 'Out of the mouths of babes and sucklings thou hast perfected praise?' " (Matt. 21:16).

When Jesus made this statement, He revealed one of the secrets of praise; in its purest form, it is a very simple child*like* (not child*ish*) act. Man, with his religious ways, seems to delight in complicating the truths of God. However, God's ways are very simple.

The Lord, speaking through the prophet Isaiah, referred to the way of holiness in the following manner: "The unclean shall not pass over it; but it shall be for those: the wayfaring men, though fools, shall not err therein" (Isa. 35:8). If, in childlike faith, we respond to the Word of God, He will teach us His ways. He will open our understanding, for His Word says, "The entrance of thy words giveth light; it giveth understanding unto the simple" (Ps.119:130).

The Last Supper

The Hallel, or Hymn of Praise, is a series of six Psalms (Ps. 113-118) sung by the Jews in times of festivity, especially during the feasts of passover, pentecost, and tabernacles. The hymn sung by Jesus and His disciples before going to the Mount of Olives was probably part of the Hallel. Just before Jesus gave His life, He and His disciples lifted their voices in an anthem of praise unto the Father (Matt. 26:30). No matter the circumstances of our lives, we too, should continually offer to God anthems of praise, that from our lives would flow one great "Hallel" unto Him.

Pentecost

After Jesus ascended into heaven, the disciples "worshipped Him, and returned to Jerusalem with great Joy: and were continually in the temple, praising and blessing God" (Luke 24:52,53). They continued with one accord in prayer and supplication. When the day of Pentecost was fully come, they were all in one accord in one place. After the outpouring of the Holy Spirit, about three thousand souls were added to the

Church. This fast growing, new church did not complacently rest on its laurels. Instead, the people continued *steadfastly* and they continued *daily* those activities which had been important to the apostles from the time of Jesus' ascension. One of the activities which they continued was that of praising God (Acts 2:46,47). The result was that the Lord added to the Church daily such as should be saved. After we have participated in a time of seeking God and we have seen the fruit of our worship, we should not forsake those activities which were the means of producing the harvest, rather continue those activities steadfastly and daily with diligence. The result will be that the Lord will add those among us such as should be saved.

Paul and Silas

Acts 16:25 tells us when Paul and Silas were in prison they prayed and sang anthems of praise unto God. In the midst of adverse circumstances, these men offered to God the sacrifice of praise. Even though their hands and feet had been placed in stocks, they were not in bondage. Paul and Silas lifted their voices in prayer and songs of praise, and the atmosphere became charged with God's presence. An earthquake shook the foundation of the prison, opened the doors, and loosed everyone's bands. As a result of this atmosphere of deliverance, not only were the prisoners freed, but the keeper of the prison and all that were in his house were saved. Today, many of God's people are in bondage. The most powerful message in the Word of God for these people is the message of praise. If they will pray and sing praises unto God, His powerful presence will come into their circumstances, and their bondages will be removed.

Outreach to the Unbeliever

The context from which each of the Old Testament references in Romans 15:8 through 11 have been taken, is that of exalting God for His great mercy. Psalms 18 offers praise to God because He has shown great mercy to His people by avenging them of their enemies. Verse 49 states, "Therefore will I give thanks unto thee, O LORD, among the heathen, and sing praises unto thy name." Deuteronomy 32:43 declares, "Rejoice, O ye nations, with his people: for he will avenge the blood of his servants, and will render vengeance to his adversaries, and will be merciful unto his land, and to his people." Psalms 117:1 and 2 exhorts the nations to praise the Lord for His great merciful kindness and for His truth. We are a people to whom God has revealed His mercy, for while we were yet sinners Christ died for us. Although we were separated from God we heard of His love because someone sang His praises among the "Gentiles."

Hebrews 2:11 and 12 states, "For both he that sanctifieth and they who are sanctified are all of one: for which cause he is not ashamed to call them brethren, Saying, I will declare thy name unto my brethren, in the midst of the church will I sing praise unto thee." What a glorious thought, that Jesus, Himself, comes down to sing among those who gather together to extol His Name and to offer praise to the Father! Perhaps this is what is meant in Psalms 149:6 by the "high praises of God." Praising the Lord need not be all "sacrifice." Praising the Lord is glorious!

Chapter Two

Praise - A Bible Study

In this chapter, the main Scriptures on praise have been sorted and listed under several categories for the convenience of the reader. As these Scriptures are studied you will readily see that at all times, under all circumstances, and in all stations of life, God expects that His people will praise His Name. Obviously it is impossible to include every Scripture on this vast subject. However, enough references have been included so that some understanding of praise will be brought to the reader.

Praise is a Sign of Life

Isa. 38:18 For the grave cannot praise God
Isa. 38:19 The living shall praise God
Ps. 30:9 Shall the dust praise God?
Ps. 115:17 The dead praise not the LORD

When Will I Praise the Lord?

Ps. 34:1 At all times

Ps. 42:4 With a multitude that keep holyday
Ps. 45:17 Forever and ever
Ps. 104:33 While I have my being
Ps. 106:12 After deliverance
Ps. 145:2 Every day
Ps. 146:1,2 While I have my being
Ps. 119:164 Seven times a day

Who Should Praise The Lord?

Neh. 12:43 The wives and children
Neh. 5:13 All
Ps. 8:2 Babes and sucklings
Ps. 22:23 Those who fear the LORD
Ps. 69:34 Heaven and earth
Ps. 74:21 Poor and needy
Ps. 89:5 The heavens
Ps. 103:21 His ministers
Ps. 113:1 Servants of the LORD
Ps. 117:1 All nations, all people
Ps. 132:9 Saints
Ps. 22:26 They that seek him
Ps. 145:10 All God's works

Where Will I Praise The Lord?

Ps. 22:25 In the great congregation
Ps. 35:18 In the great congregation...among much people
Ps. 111:1 In the assembly
Ps. 108:3 Among the people

How Should I Praise The Lord?

Isa. 51:11 With everlasting joy
Ex. 15:20 With timbrels and with dances

2 Chron. 13:15 With shouting
2 Chron. 29:25-30 With gladness
Ps. 5:11 Shout for joy
Ps. 7:17 According to His righteousness
Ps. 9:1,2 With whole heart
Ps. 27:6 Offering sacrifices of joy and singing
Ps. 33:1-3 Singing a new song, playing skillfully with loud noise
Ps. 40:3 With a new song
Ps. 43:4 Upon the harp
Ps. 47:1 By clapping our hands and shouting with the voice of triumph
Ps. 69:30 With a song
Ps. 86:12 With all my heart
Ps. 89:1 With my mouth
Ps. 95:1 By singing and making a joyful noise
Ps. 103:1 All that is within me
Ps. 138:1,2 With my whole heart
Ps. 144:9 Upon a psaltery and an instrument of ten strings
Ps. 145:21 My mouth speaking praises
Ps. 147:7 Upon the harp

Why Praise The Lord?

Ps. 9:14 As a testimony to His people
Ps. 18:3 He is worthy
Ps. 50:23 To glorify Him
Ps. 63:3,4 Because His lovingkindness is better than life
Ps. 67:3,4 Because of His righteous judgments
Ps. 92:1-4 It is a good thing to give thanks...and sing praise
Ps. 102:18 We were created to praise the LORD

What Does Praise Produce?

2 Chron. 5:13 Glory
2 Chron. 15:14,15 Rest
2 Chron. 20:19-21 Ambushments
Ps. 22:3 The Presence of God
Acts 16:25-31 Deliverance

To Wait on The Lord is to Praise The Lord

Isa. 40:31 They that wait upon the LORD shall renew
their strength
Isa. 41:1 The people renew their strength
Ps. 65:1 Praise waiteth for thee, O God
Isa. 14:7 The whole earth is at rest, and is quiet: they
break forth into singing

Praise in Restoration

Ezra 3:10,11,13 At the rebuilding of the temple
Neh. 12:43 At the dedication of the walls of Jerusalem

Chapter Three

Spiritual Sacrifices

One problem encountered by those teaching the message of praise is frequently expressed in the following manner: "I don't want to be a hypocrite. If I raise my hands during praise and worship when I do not feel like praising the Lord, then I am a hypocrite. I am not praising from my heart, I am just making a noise and God does not receive that!" There is an element of truth in this statement, because it is possible to slide into a form of praise when screaming, "Hallelujah! Praise the Lord!", while our minds are a million miles away. I do not believe God honors this. However, there is another aspect of the message of praise, that of knowing we are spiritual priests unto the Lord, and that God is pleased when we sacrifice unto Him.

In Old Testament times, people brought the very best of their substance and presented it unto the Lord as an offering. They presented sacrificial animals to the priests, who slew the animals upon the altar. The shedding of the blood of these animals was accepted as a covering for sin. Today we do not bring sacrificial animals to church with us. We do not have altars where animals might be slain and offered unto the Lord, because the Word of God tells us that all blood sacrifice was done away with at Calvary where Jesus became the final sacrifice for sin.

Although the need for *blood* sacrifice was fulfilled at Calvary, the principle of sacrifice was not abolished. The principle of sacrifice originates in the heart of God. Because man was created in God's image, within every human being there is a desire to sacrifice. One individual who touched this principle of sacrifice was David, who also touched God's principle of abundance. He realized the more abundantly he sacrificed, the more abundant was the touch of God upon His people and upon his own life. David said, "I will *freely* sacrifice unto thee" (Ps. 54:6). Today, God loves a cheerful giver, not only of finances, but also of every spiritual sacrifice. David also realized that God is not pleased with the offering of that which has cost him nothing. He said, "Neither will I offer burnt offerings unto the LORD my God of that which doth cost me nothing" (2 Sam. 24:24).

God is bound by His Word to meet His people when they sacrifice unto Him. This principle holds true throughout the Word of God. When the patriarchs desired to meet with God, they built an alter, knowing that if they would have God's presence, they must sacrifice. Abraham, Jacob, and Elijah were three men who built alters, and God never failed to meet with them. We, too, must prepare an altar and a sacrifice in order that we might meet with God: not a literal altar upon which we might sacrifice animals, but a spiritual altar upon which we might offer spiritual sacrifices unto God.

First Peter 2:5 declares, "Ye also, as lively stones, are built up a spiritual house, an holy priesthood, to offer up spiritual sacrifices, acceptable to God by Jesus Christ." First Peter 2:9 tells us that we are a royal priesthood. As a royal priesthood, *we* become priests, and *we* offer sacrifices acceptable unto the Lord. The initial experience of salvation does not involve too much sacrifice on the part of the new believer, yet there is some. We sacrifice worldly pleasures, habits, friends, and even finances, in order to walk with God. As our relationship with God grows, our ability to sacrifice expands, for with each experience in God comes an increasingly greater challenge to sacrifice, both naturally and spiritually. Together, as living stones, we are being built into a spiritual house, into a holy priesthood, for the purpose of offering spiritual sacrifices unto the Lord. Therefore, we have not eliminated sacrifice, but rather our sacrifice has changed. No longer do we offer to God blood sacrifices or meal offerings according to the standard of the Old Testament law, but we do come before God as spiritual kings and priests, offering to Him spiritual sacrifices which are acceptable to God by Jesus Christ (1 Pet. 2:5). This chapter will present several spiritual sacrifices, discussing their role in the worship of New Testament kings and priests.

The Sacrifices of God

Psalms 51:17 states, "The sacrifices of God are a

broken spirit: a broken and a contrite heart, O God, thou wilt not despise." True spiritual sacrifice is offered from a heart that has been broken by the love of God, for a heart that has been bowed low before the Lord is pleasing unto Him. Even during the days of Old Testament sacrifice, David received a revelation of the last-day Church which would bring sacrifices pleasing to the heart of God. Never at any time did the sacrifice of bulls and goats please God; they only appeased Him. Psalms 40:6 states, "Sacrifice and offering thou didst not desire; mine ears hast thou opened: burnt offering and sin offering has thou not required." When the Church moves in the realm of spiritual sacrifice, God's heart is pleased.

This, then, answers a frequently asked question: "If I praise when I do not feel like praising, am I a hypocrite?" The answer is "No." There have been times in my life when to offer praise to God was the most difficult thing I knew to do. At those times I did not feel like praising the Lord. I did not want to praise the Lord. All I wanted was "to do my own thing." However, because I loved God, because I was able to say, "God, even if my flesh does not want to praise You, my heart has been broken by Your love and I will do what Your Word tells me to do," I was lifted from the realm of hypocrisy into the realm of faith. My flesh said, "I will worship the way I want to," but my broken heart said, "Not my will, but Thine be done. I will praise You, Lord, because my heart has been bowed before You, and You have broken my heart with Your love."

The Living Sacrifice

Another sacrifice which is pleasing to God is the

living sacrifice of our bodies. Some people would like to crawl upon the altar and say to the pastor, "Smite me through the heart and then it will be all over!" Many times it would be easier to be a dead sacrifice. However, God's Son was smitten on Calvary, and on this side of Calvary, He desires a living sacrifice. God desires that daily we present our bodies unto Him as living sacrifices. Everything we do must become an expression of praise and worship unto Him (Rom. 12:1)

Becoming a living sacrifice involves complete abdication of our own rights, for involved in being a living sacrifice is our service to the Body of Christ. God may call upon us for service to His Body whenever it pleases Him. We must abdicate the right to our time, our pleasure, and our finances, and enter into a realm of complete dependence upon God for the supply of both our spiritual and our natural needs. In order to become a living sacrifice, as was Jesus Christ, the theme of our lives must be "I HAVE NO RIGHTS...I BELONG TO HIM WHO HAS PURCHASED ME!" The sacrifice does not matter, if only it pleases Him for Whose pleasure we were created!

> *I was born to be Your dwelling place,*
> *A home for the presence of the Lord.*
> *Let my heart now be separated unto Thee,*
> *That I may be what I was born to be!"*

The Sacrifice of Praise

The sacrifice of praise is a spiritual sacrifice which we offer to God continually: "By him therefore let us offer the sacrifice of praise to God continually, that is, the fruit of our lips giving thanks to his name" (Heb. 13:15).

If our hearts have been broken by His love, and if we have become a living sacrifice, then praise will naturally flow from our lips. This does not mean that we audibly say, "Hallelujah, Praise the Lord," continually when we are at work or among the unsaved, but it does mean that praise has become a twenty-four-hour-per-day life style. A blessing is something *we receive* when we come into the house of God, study His Word, or pray. The sacrifice of praise is something *we bring with us* which we may offer to God, not on the basis of feelings or circumstances, but on the basis of a revelation of the greatness of God, a desire to please Him and to be obedient to His Word.

Occasionally someone will say, "My nature is not to be noisy. I do not want to yell and scream and make a big noise. I will praise the Lord silently in my heart." However, the Scripture instructs that the sacrifice of praise involves the fruit of our lips. Psalms 66:8 declares, "O bless our God, ye people, and *make the voice of his praise to be heard.*" If we wish to give God the fruit of our lips, then we must audibly praise Him. When we audibly praise God, we create an atmosphere in which He is pleased to dwell. The more we praise God, the more we have of His presence; the less we praise Him, the less of His presence will dwell among us. However, let it be noted that nowhere in the Word does God indicate that He is pleased when we copy another person's mannerisms or volume of praise. We are to give God *our own* sacrifice of praise, which is the heart expression of the unique new creation, the believer.

Romans 10:17 presents a basic principle of faith: "So then faith cometh by hearing, and hearing by the word of God." When we praise God audibly, our ears hear what our mouths are saying, our hearts respond, and faith is created. This is why we are to speak positive words. This is why we want to fill our homes and our lives with audible praise and this is why we should become comfortable praising the Lord. If we praise God only during a public service, we leave a good portion of the sense of God's presence when we depart. When we offer the sacrifice of praise to God *continually*, we not only surround ourselves with an atmosphere in which God is pleased to dwell, but we also receive an infusion of faith, the enablement to praise Him more and more.

There are times when one may come to the house of the Lord not feeling like praising God. At those times, the natural tendency to sit back and think, "I will not be a hypocrite." This is a wrong concept. Our flesh is to be brought into subjection to the Word of God. We are to say, "Flesh, stand there and do what the Word of God commands, for the Bible says: "My mouth shall speak the praise of the LORD" (Ps. 145:21). Indeed, the Word of the Lord does declare, "Bless the LORD, O my soul: and all that is within me, bless his holy name" (Ps. 103:1). Although we may be in a turmoil and may not feel like praising Him, when we bring the sacrifice which God says is acceptable to Him, God responds. He enters into that atmosphere of praise and dwells there. Then after church we find ourselves saying, "Why on earth was I angry? Why was I so sour when I came to church? I feel fulfilled and happy now. What happened? I have financial problems. My car does not run. My bank account is empty. I need a job. Yet I feel great! What has happened?"

When you chose to subject your attitudes, your fatigue, and your circumstances to the Word of God, He was pleased. There is not a better thing your flesh can do than praise God. When flesh begins to rise up, make it praise the Lord! The first thing you know, your temper will have gone below the boiling point, and your tongue will have gone back where it belongs. You will not find yourself talking about your neighbor, but you will be praising the Lord! It is difficult to criticize your neighbor and praise the Lord at the same time!

Some people are an offence because all they do is yell and scream. Although they make much noise, their hearts are not involved. I do not believe in doing that. We must come honestly before the Lord, saying, "God, with my faults and failures, with my needs, my problems, my flesh, and my humanity, with everything that I am, I will praise You because You are God. I will praise You because Your Word tells me that praise is pleasing to You." God wants a people who will say, "Lord, this flesh must be brought into control before I can become a worshipper. I want to harness my flesh. I want to harness my spirit. I want to learn to live in the presence of God."

It must be noted here that mere mortal man can never "create the presence of God". Praise is only the means by which we create the *atmosphere* in which God loves to dwell. The basis of our praise is not feelings or circumstances, but rather on the basis of

(a) His eternal word

(b) His eternal worthiness.

There are times when we enter the sanctuary and it is the pleasure of the Holy Spirit that we stand and praise the Lord. Often when this happens, someone will say, "Church was not too spiritual tonight. All we did was praise the Lord. We did not have deep worship." Let it not be said that the realm of praise is "less spiritual" than the realm of worship. True worship cannot exist until the worshippers have first experienced praise. The most important thing is not to enter into "deep worship" every service, but rather that we will do the thing that pleases God for that service. Perhaps the thing that would please the heart of God is that we would stand and praise Him, saying, "God, You are good. I love You. It is good to be a Christian. Hallelujah!"

Frequently when a congregation begins to praise the Lord, the praise will start on the level of the sacrifice of praise. The people raise their hands and say, "Jesus, we love You. From the rising of the sun to the going down of the same, Thy Name is to be praised." As the Spirit of God comes down upon the congregation, people are lifted into another dimension of praise. God accepted the sacrifice offered to Him by the congregation, and when He accepted that sacrifice, His presence became very real. Praising the Lord is not empty form. It is the outward expression of a relationship in which we desire to magnify the Name of the Lord.

The Sacrifice of Doing Good and Communication

One of the problems of humanity is the tendency to lay hold on part of a Scripture which pleases us, but we drop the rest. For example, someone will say, "I am a praiser! Hallelujah," but will not work in the natural areas of the church, or "I would help Brother Jones, but I am tired and I want to relax." However, God says,

"But to *do good* and to *communicate* forget not: for with such sacrifices God is well pleased" (Heb. 13:16). Working with a shovel, hammer, or dustcloth may not seem like sacrifices, but they *are* spiritual sacrifices. We can be spiritual while ministering to the natural areas of the Body of Christ, because our work becomes a spiritual sacrifice unto the Lord.

Not only are we to remember the sacrifice of doing good, but we must remember the sacrifice of communication. We are to communicate with one another. When was the last time you communicated your faith to someone? When was the last time you went to someone who was having a hard time financially and said, "I really believe that Jehovah-jireh is your provider and that He will supply your need," perhaps even giving of your finances to help. At times we notice people in difficult situations when we, ourselves, are in a tight spot. At these times we are tempted to say, "Well, I am just not in the mood to help that person." If we are feeling this way, then we have a unique opportunity to offer the spiritual sacrifice of communication.

In Romans 10:8 we read, "Thy word is nigh thee, even in thy mouth, and in thy heart: that is, the word of faith, which we preach." This leads us to believe that faith is activated by the spoken word. Even though this may involve a real sacrifice on the part of one who speaks faith, on many occasions I have seen the spoken word of faith become active in a life, causing miracles to occur. Speaking the word of faith is also involved in the sacrifice of communication.

The Sacrifice of Thanksgiving

Psalms 107:21 and 22 states, "Oh that men would praise the LORD for his goodness, and for his wonderful works to the children of men! And let them sacrifice the sacrifices of thanksgiving, and declare his works with rejoicing." The scriptural way to testify is with the voice of thanksgiving: "Lord, I *thank you* for this trial. I thank You for every experience of life. My flesh does not want to thank You. My mind does not want to thank You, but I am ordering everything within me to sacrifice thanksgiving unto my God." When the world can see men who are thankful *in* everything and are rejoicing in God in the midst of their circumstances, they will believe!

"I will offer to thee the sacrifice of thanksgiving, and will call upon the name of the LORD" (Ps. 116:17). When we are in need, we are to thank God BEFORE the answer comes, and then call upon His Name. Many Christians are going around and around in their circumstances because they have never learned the secret of sacrificing thanksgiving.

Jonah was in terrible circumstances with no cause for thanksgiving, but he declared, "But I will sacrifice unto thee with the voice of thanksgiving" (Jon. 2:9). Even here, God's presence in Jonah was greater than Jonah's flesh, and he refused to let his spirit be bound.

Chapter 2 of Jonah tells us how he tried to escape his circumstances, but his attempts were of no avail. Jonah repented, he cried unto God and he confessed that he was not observing lying vanities; none of these confessions produced a change in his circumstances. When he sacrificed to God with the voice of thanksgiving,

IMMEDIATELY the fish become ill! A thankful prophet was too much for the fish!

I do not know how we would feel if we were sitting inside the rib cage of a fish, encased in seaweed and being slowly digested! I do not know how many of us would have faith to say, "Yet thou hast brought up my life from corruption, O LORD my God...I will sacrifice unto thee with the voice of thanksgiving" (Jon. 1:6-9). In that dire circumstance Jonah decided to lift his voice and sacrifice thanksgiving to his God. I have looked at this example many times and have said, "God, I am not in circumstances as terrible as Jonah's. If he could thank You in his situation, then I can thank You in mine."

God's people should never stop expressing thanksgiving. Second Timothy 3:2 tells us that one of the signs of the last generation is a people who are unthankful. Thanklessness is part of the spirit of this age. In the Church we tend to take God for granted or we thank Him for all His goodness and rebuke the things which we do not like. "I thank You for my nice car, my nice family, my nice house, and all of the nice things which You have given to me, but I rebuke this other thing in the Name of Jesus, I do not like it." All the time we are rebuking, God is waiting to hear the voice of thanksgiving. The sacrifice of thanksgiving is not thanking God when we feel like it, but it involves the *sacrifice* of being thankful. When we learn the secret of the sacrifice of thanksgiving, we touch something that is pleasing to the heart of God.

"In every thing give thanks: for this is the will of God in Christ Jesus concerning you" (1 Thess. 5:18). It is easy to be thankful when we feel we have something to be thankful for, but giving God the sacrifice of thanksgiving involves giving thanks for everything. Because we know every step in the life of the Spirit-led Christian has been ordained of God for good and not for evil, even the most adverse circumstances cause us to lift our voices and thank God. This sacrifice is pleasing to God.

"And when ye will offer a sacrifice of thanksgiving unto the LORD, offer it at your own will" (Lev. 22:29). Even under the law God instituted the sacrifice of thanksgiving. When Israel was to bring an offering of thanksgiving, God specifically said, "You will bring it of your own free will." There were some things Israel was commanded to do; they had no choice. When it came to thanksgiving, God told them they must bring their free will into operation. We do not offer the sacrifices of thanksgiving because somebody has told us to be thankful, but because we have seen this principle in the Word of God and our hearts have been broken by His love. Because of these things, we can say, "Lord, thank You for this difficult situation. I am encased by circumstances. Everywhere I look, I see the 'rib cage of the fish.' I do not understand how Jonah could pray toward Your holy temple, or how he found his direction but by faith in God he found his way! Therefore I will sacrifice to Thee with a voice of thanksgiving."

Sacrificing to God with a voice of thanksgiving does not mean that the thanksgiving is given only in the heart. Sacrificing to God with the *voice* of thanksgiving means that the thanksgiving is spoken. Audible thanksgiving puts a very simple principle into operation, the principle of the hearing ear and the believing heart. When I think to myself, my ears are not hearing anything. They are not being digged by the Spirit of God. The Word of God says, "faith cometh by hearing" (Rom. 10:17). When we sacrifice with the *voice* of thanksgiving, our ears hear what our mouth declares. Faith is produced in our hearts. Faith is our deliverance, for nothing can change a circumstance like faith. The minute Jonah sacrificed unto the Lord with the voice of thanksgiving, the fish became ill and headed for shore! There are many people swimming around in the sea of their own circumstances. If they would offer to God the Sacrifice of thanksgiving with the voice of thanksgiving, their fish would head for shore and they would be set free!

The Sacrifice of Joy

"And now shall mine head be lifted up above mine enemies round about me: therefore will I offer in his tabernacle sacrifices of joy; I will sing, yea, I will sing praises unto the Lord" (Ps. 27:6). The original rendering of "sacrifices of joy" is, "I will offer sacrifices of SHOUTING," indicating there is a spiritual sacrifice which involves literally shouting aloud our joy in Him. This sacrifice causes us to deny our natural "religious" nature, which is to be quiet. Psalms 47:5 tells us that God has gone up with a shout. First Thessalonians 4:16 tells us that God is coming back with a shout. In the meantime, the Church is commanded to shout! If we do not feel like shouting, the Bible tells us there is a way for us to be acceptable unto God, and that is to stand and shout the victory. There is one thing we all can do with a whole heart, and that is to make a joyful *noise* unto the Lord...to shout unto the Lord with a voice of triumph. We must learn to rejoice *in God* and to find Him as our joy. Even if we do not feel like shouting, God is pleased because His priests are offering a spiritual sacrifice unto Him.

There is a difference between the joy of the Lord and a naturally joyful, exuberant spirit. Some people are naturally happy and outgoing in their nature; there is no sacrifice involved in their expression of joy. Those who are not of this disposition, find it difficult to enter into the aspect of praise which involves the expression of joy. For these people, the expression of joy is a sacrifice, but as priests unto God, they must offer to Him this expression.

"Blessed are ye, when men shall hate you, and when they shall separate you from their company, and shall reproach you, and cast out your name as evil, for the Son of man's sake. Rejoice ye in that day, and leap for joy: for, behold, your reward is great in heaven: for in the like manner did their fathers unto the prophets" (Luke 6:22,23). The last day church will be reviled, evil spoken of, persecuted and ridiculed for the message they proclaim. Such a people will not be sad and downcast but will literally leap for joy at the thought of suffering for His Name! Certainly this will be the sacrifice of joy.

Included in the sacrifice of joy, is dancing before the Lord. "Let them praise His name in the dance" (Ps. 149:3). When the will of God for a service involves dancing, we should dance. We should rejoice before the Lord, expressing our joy in Him. The day may come when we will need this liberty. Although we may not feel like rejoicing, the sacrifice which we offer when we are obedient to the Word of God will produce true joy in our hearts.

The Sacrifices of Righteousness

Deuteronomy 33:19 and Psalms 51:19 speak of the sacrifices (plural) of righteousness. There are many sacrifices of righteousness. Righteousness is a state of being "right" before God, knowing that in each realm of challenge presented to us by His Word we have made ourselves "right" by the enablement of His Holy Spirit. At salvation we offered to God the sacrifice of righteousness when we turned our backs upon sin in order to walk with Jesus. The sacrifice of righteousness was also involved at the Baptism of the Holy Spirit. Each succeeding visitation of God involves sacrifice on our part. With each revelation of truth, God demands a higher standard of righteousness from His people.

The sacrifices of righteousness may also be experienced individually in our daily lives. It is not easy for a person to be one hundred percent righteous, one hundred percent of the time. However, there are times when you may offer a spiritual sacrifice of being righteous unto the Lord. If the church calls a fast and you say, "Well! I have good reason for not fasting. I do not want to fast. I will fast next week," you may speak to yourself and say, "Self, you are going to fast. God's people are fasting and praying, and I am going to fast and pray. Flesh, I will bring you into subjection, and offer to God a sacrifice of righteousness." When we make a decision to do what is right in the sight of God and trust the Lord for His enablement, God honors that decision as a spiritual sacrifice, and we as priests offer upon an altar a sacrifice which is acceptable unto Him.

The Sacrifice and Service of Faith

The apostle Paul said, "Yea, and if I be offered upon the sacrifice and service of your faith, I joy and rejoice with you all" (Phil. 2:17). The ministry must always be the firstfruits of each truth God restores. Paul is saying that any sacrifice which he may be called upon to make in the service of faith is not grievous, but is a means of obtaining true joy. Too many times truth is birthed in the Church congregation, but is not birthed in the ministry. This happens as a matter of expediency rather than of principle. Many of God's good pastors are missing the great joy involved in this sacrifice.

As new truth is restored to the Church, ministries with vision may suffer much for the birthing of that truth in the church. There is no greater joy than being involved in the bringing forth of new truth, which will bless the Body of Christ.

Psalms 50:5 declares, "Gather my saints together unto me; those that have made a covenant with me by sacrifice." In the last days God will have a company of people who have entered into a covenant relationship with Him which is signified by sacrifice. This will be a company of priests who will offer spiritual sacrifices unto the Lord. Today we may not feel like being righteous, praising the Lord, or communicating, but as priests we offer these sacrifices unto Him. Psalms 103:1 states, "Bless the LORD, O my soul..." Therefore, our position is not that God blesses *us*, but it is that we bless Him. God is pleased with the sacrifices which we bring unto Him.

Part Two

The Message of Worship

"Extravagant Love and Extreme Submission"

Chapter Four

Worship

Several words have been translated "worship" in the Old and New Testament. The Hebrew word most frequently translated "worship" means "to depress, to prostrate oneself in homage to royalty or to God." The Greek word most frequently translated "worship" means "to fawn or crouch to, to prostrate oneself in homage, to do reverence to, or to adore." This Greek word is taken from a word meaning "to kiss, like a dog licking his master's hand." These definitions indicate that worship not only involves relationship between an inferior and a superior, but worship also involves a love relationship. When we worship the Lord, we prostrate ourselves before Him in total submission (not always physically, but in spirit), giving reverence to Him, and pouring out upon Him our deep love. Just as a dog follows his master in order that he might be in his master's presence, so will the true worshipper follow Jesus. Nothing means more to the true worshipper than being in the presence of the Lord.

Not only is worship dependent upon our relationship with God, but it is also dependent upon our relationship with the Body of Christ. If we are angry or harbor bitterness, hatred, and criticism, our love for God will be dissipated. True worship can only flow from a heart that has been cleansed through times of deep repentance.

Reverence for the greatness of God and the desire to exalt and glorify His Name are involved in worship. As we come into the presence of God, the Holy Spirit begins to minister to us. As we respond and begin to exalt Him, we realize how small our problems are and how great the Lord really is! A problem with which we have been wrestling for months may be taken care of during one session of true worship.

Finally, worship involves our total life style. Worship requires that we give our strength unto the Lord (Ps. 29:1). Paul declares in Romans 12:1, "I beseech you therefore, brethren, by the mercies of God, that ye present your bodies a living sacrifice, holy, acceptable unto God, which is your reasonable service." Every act should be an act of worship so that we (spirit, soul, and body) might be poured out as worship unto God.

Differences Between Praise and Worship

Praise, an operation of faith, is an instrument which will create the atmosphere for the presence of God, where He is pleased to dwell (Ps. 22:3). Praise is often used in times of need, discouragement, testing, temptation or warfare, creating the atmosphere of praise in the midst of our circumstances in order that our lives might be fortified against the work of the enemy. In contrast, worship is the expression of our response to

His presence. Worship involves relationship and response and receiving of His life and His anointing. Some people who ardently participate in praise services, become uncomfortable during times when the congregation bows before Jesus, expressing love for Him. These people do not possess that love relationship with God which is expressed in response to His presence.

Praise often involves sacrifice. At times we offer to God the sacrifice of praise (Heb. 13:15). However, *true worship* does not involve sacrifice, for the Bible does not mention the "sacrifice of *worship*." We do not give God the sacrifice of love. We either love Him or we do not. We either worship Him because we love Him, or we do not worship Him at all. Many people who have been saved and filled with the Holy Spirit, do not have a love relationship with Jesus. True worship is not a part of their lives.

We cannot be true worshippers until we have first had an experience in praise. When two people are in love, they begin to talk about each other, extolling each other's virtues, and their speech indicates that a love relationship is developing. The same is true of our relationship with Jesus. As we learn to know Him, we begin to extol His virtues. We begin to audibly praise His Name. As our relationship with Jesus deepens, our worship increases. Gradually we learn to know Him in a more intimate way, and we pour out our hearts unto Him in worship.

Physical expressions of worship and praise, such as lifting of hands, the clapping of hands, dancing, and prostrating oneself before the Lord, are expressions specifically mentioned in the Bible. We feel these expressions are a part of worship in the restored Church today. However, it should be noted that the physical expression without the proper attitude of heart, is completely meaningless and even hypocritical.

One distinction which is often made when the natural mind tries to analyze the moving of the Spirit of God, is that of labeling part of a worship service *praise* and another part *worship*. We often call slow songs worship and fast songs praise. There have been times when the Spirit of God has swept over our congregation and we have bowed low in His presence. Other times we have rejoiced before the Lord singing, dancing, and pouring out upon Him our love and joy. In God's eyes, both are worship. The important distinction between praise and worship is not the particular expression which is manifested in a service, but the fact that while praise is often operated as *an act of faith* creating the atmosphere for the presence of God, worship is *the expression of our response* to His presence.

The words "vertical" and "horizontal" may be used in making a distinction between praise and worship. For maximum understanding of the material presented in this book, the reader must differentiate between these two concepts. The sacrifice of praise is geared to time, relating to the believer in each and every situation of his daily life. Praise is born of faith, is an instrument of war and a method of creating an atmosphere for the presence of God. We often offer to God the sacrifice of praise in order that He will bless, help, deliver, and dwell with us so that on earth we might reign as overcomers. Praise, therefore, is "horizontal," applying to the daily life of the believer here on earth. Worship, the expression of an eternal relationship, is "vertical." Born from the womb of our relationship with God, worship involves our response to His divine presence. Worship is never ending, and ever increasing, for our relationship with God will grow throughout eternity.

Excellence in Worship

When we gather in the house of God, we are united through worship, the seedbed of all creative expression. As we worship the Lord, He pours His life into us that in everything we do, we might be channels of His life. The purpose of expressive worship is that we might bring pleasure unto God, and offer our bodies as living sacrifices unto Him, for Romans 12:1 and 2 states, "I beseech you therefore, brethren, by the mercies of God, that ye present your bodies a living sacrifice, holy, acceptable unto God, which is your reasonable service. And be not conformed to this world:..."

First Peter 2:9 tells us that we are a royal priesthood chosen for the purpose of showing forth the praises of God. (The word "praises" has been translated from a Greek word meaning "manliness, valor, or excellence.") God desires a people who will produce a standard of excellence. His Name is excellent (Ps. 8:1), His glory is excellent (2 Pet. 1:17) and His instruction is excellent (Rom. 2:18). The Church is beginning to see that God is a God Who desires His people to worship Him with excellence. Revelation 4:11 declares that we are created that we might bring pleasure unto Him by showing forth the excellence of His Name.

Today people of great talent and training in the creative arts are being saved and filled with the Holy Spirit. These people are expressing God in ways which might have been unacceptable a few years ago. When God moves upon them, they become channels through which His Glory is expressed in their individual areas of creative ability. For those who have been trained to dance, this is a medium through which they are able to express God. Those who have been trained to sing can abandon themselves in song. Others will move in their fields of artistic expression. We must each find the unique abilities God has put within our lives in order that we might express God in excellence. Expressive worship includes the areas of dancing, art, music, architecture, law, teaching, sculpture, and handicrafts. God will sanctify the abilities which have been deposited within His people in order that they might be acceptable expressions of worship in the house of the Lord.

One problem associated with expressive worship is imitation; that is, one person attempting to imitate another person's expression. Just as violins do not imitate drums or wind instruments, we should not imitate each other. A stringed instrument might be able to produce a sound *similar* to a wind instrument, but instruments which are plucked or bowed, will never replace those which are blown upon. So it is with the expression of the deposit which God has placed within the lives of His people. We are to do what God has called us to do. God has deposited a portion of Himself within each one of His people; this deposit must be expressed.

Today, God is conforming every area of our lives unto His Word. He is causing excellence to be manifested in the house of the Lord. When the King rides into Jerusalem the Church will be glorious. She will be beautiful when He comes for her! In that day, a symphony of worship will be offered unto the Lord. United through the guidance of the Holy Spirit, God-appointed ministries, and the Word, God's people will flow together in excellence, worshipping Him in Spirit and in Truth!

Chapter Five

Bowing in Worship

Throughout the Bible, reference is made to bowing or prostrating oneself before the Lord. This concept of worship is presented in Genesis, developed throughout the Word of God, and culminated in the book of Revelation as true worshippers of the Lamb prostrate themselves in worship before Him.

Abraham

Genesis 18:1 tells us that the Lord appeared unto Abraham in the plains of Mamre. When the three men approached Abraham in the heat of the day, Abraham immediately bowed himself toward the ground. There must have been a manifestation indicating to Abraham that he was in the presence of God. When God's people experience His presence or a manifestation of His glory, they desire to prostrate themselves before Him.

Today, it is not usual for people to prostrate themselves before the Lord. Often their attitude is not that of bowing. As God's people learn to know Him more intimately, and as they begin to experience an increasing awareness of His presence, they will literally bow themselves in worship before Him.

Lot

Genesis 19:1 tells us that when the two angels came to tell Lot of the impending destruction and judgment of Sodom, Lot bowed himself with his face toward the ground. Again, we see a bowing low in the presence of the Lord.

Eliezer

Eliezer, the eldest servant in the house of Abraham, had been sent to find a bride for Isaac. Abraham's instructions to Eliezer were, "Go unto my country, and to my kindred, and take a wife unto my son Isaac. The Lord God of heaven...shall send his angel before thee, and thou shalt take a wife unto my son from thence" (Gen. 24:4-7). Eliezer set out on his journey. When Eliezer entered the city of Nahor, he stood by a well and asked the Lord to bring Isaac's appointed bride unto him. It came to pass that the Lord brought Rebekah, the daughter of Bethuel, unto Eliezer. When Eliezer realized that Rebekah was the woman whom God intended to be Isaac's bride, he bowed his head and worshipped the Lord, saying "Blessed be the LORD God of my master Abraham, who hath not left destitute my master of his mercy and his truth: I being in the way, the LORD led me to the house of my master's brethren" (v.27). The fact that Eliezer was standing by a well in the city of Nahor did not deter him from bowing his head and prostrating himself before the

Lord. So grateful was Eliezer for the accomplishment of his master's command, he worshipped God!

There are times when the Lord, or even those in ministry over us, will ask of us what seems to be an impossible task. At those times the Lord will not leave us destitute. If we obey the instructions given to us, we will find that God will send an angel before us to lead us in the right way. When we see the purpose of our journey fulfilled, we are to bow our heads and worship the Lord, giving glory unto Him.

The Children of Israel

For many years the children of Israel had been afflicted in the land of Egypt. Although they had cried unto the Lord, they received no indication the Lord had heard their prayers. When Moses and Aaron presented the word of the Lord unto Israel with signs and wonders, the people knew God had heard their cry. They knew the Lord would fulfill the deepest desire of their hearts, setting them free from that land of bitterness and bondage. Therefore, upon hearing the word of the Lord and seeing the signs which the Lord performed, through Moses, the people bowed their heads and worshipped the Lord (Ex. 4:30-31). So grateful were the children of Israel when they heard of the visitation of the Lord, that they bowed their heads and prostrated themselves before Him. What a pleasure that must have been unto God — the sight of an entire nation bowed low before His presence!

Exodus 12 presents the account of the Lord giving Israel instructions for the feast of the Passover. After He finished, the Lord told the people to tell their children the purpose of the Passover: "It is the sacrifice of the LORD's passover, who passed over the houses of the children of Israel in Egypt, when he smote the Egyptians, and delivered our houses. And the people bowed their heads and worshipped'' (Ex. 12:27). Again we see an example of the entire nation of Israel prostrating themselves before the God of their salvation.

Moses

Exodus 34:1 through 9 gives an account of the proclamation of the Name of the Lord unto Moses. What was the proclamation of the Name of the Lord? What were the results of this proclamation? How does this event relate to the Church today? In order to understand its significance, we must examine the events immediately preceding and following the proclamation of the Name of the Lord to Moses.

The first thing the Lord told Moses was "Hew thee two tables of stone like unto the first: and I will write upon these tables the words that were in the first tables, which thou brakest'' (v.1). Before the proclamation of the Name of the Lord took place, Moses was told to prepare for the restoration of the Word of the Lord. Today the Word of the Lord is written not on stones but upon the fleshly tables of the heart (2 Cor. 3:3). We must prepare our hearts to receive a new portion of the Word of God. Part of this preparation involves repentance. Psalms 119:136 states, "Rivers of waters run down mine eyes, because they keep not thy law.'' Unto a broken hearted and repentant people God will restore His Word!

The second instruction given to Moses by the Lord was: "And be ready in the morning, and come up in the morning unto mount Sinai, and present thyself there to me in the top of the mount" (Ex. 34:2). Throughout the night season, God has been preparing a people who will enter into the new day. Those who have yielded to the dealings of the Holy Spirit, will have prepared themselves to meet the new day and all that it contains. At the dawning of that new day, God's people will present themselves before the Lord.

Next, the Lord said to Moses, "And no man shall come up with thee, neither let any man be seen throughout all the mount;" (v.3). Today the Spirit of God is seeking a solitary people who will ascend the mountain at the break of day. When God calls His people to the mountain of revelation at the dawning of the new day, He will be calling them unto Himself. God wants to proclaim His Name unto a solitary people.

Finally, the Lord said, "Neither let the flocks nor herds feed before that mount" (v.3). Flocks and herds were not to feed before that mountain of worship and personal encounter with the Lord. Material possessions have no hold upon the true worshipper — "flocks and herds" cannot feed before that mount. God does not want His people to be poverty-stricken, but neither can one be a lover of His presence, a worshipper, and be in bondage to the god of this world, material possessions.

Moses obeyed the command of the Lord. He rose early in the morning and ascended mount Sinai, taking the two tables of stone with him (Ex. 34:4). When Moses ascended the mount, the Lord descended in the cloud and stood with him. The Lord passed by, proclaiming the Name of the Lord, and immediately following the proclamation of that Name, Moses bowed his head toward the earth and worshipped. As he worshipped, he began to make intercession for God's people. He asked that the Lord go among them. Moses wanted Israel to experience more than just a visitation of God's presence, he wanted them to experience His abiding presence. Next, Moses confessed the sin of Israel and asked forgiveness. Finally, Moses asked the Lord to take Israel for His inheritance. In Deuteronomy 4:20, we see his prayer answered: "But the LORD hath taken you, and brought you forth out of the iron furnace, even out of Egypt, to be unto him a people of inheritance, as ye are this day."

After Moses worshipped the Lord and made intercession for the people, the Lord made a covenant with Israel. "And he said, Behold, I make a covenant: before all thy people I will do marvels, such as have not been done in all the earth, nor in any nation: and all the people among which thou art shall see the work of the LORD" (Ex. 34:10). As part of this covenant, the Lord said He would drive out the Amorite, and Canaanite, the Hittite, the Perizzite, the Hivite, and the Jebusite. He also said he would cast out the nations before His people, and enlarge the borders of Israel (v.24).

There is coming a day when the Lord Himself will proclaim His Name before a prepared people. Accompanying this proclamation will be restoration of the Word of the Lord and a personal encounter with God for each person who ascends the mountain. Those who hear the proclamation of His Name will fall to the earth in worship. Part of this worship will involve making intercession for all of God's people! As a result, the Church upon whom the presence of God rests will overcome the nations of the earth wherever she goes, destroying altars, breaking down images, and cutting down groves of the heathen gods. Into the nations of the earth will God extend the borders of the Church which He has encountered upon the mountain and before whom He has proclaimed His Name.

Joshua

After the death of Moses, God revealed Himself to Joshua (Josh. 5:13-15). God met Joshua according to the ministry to which he had been called. He did not reveal Himself to Joshua as the "Lion of Judah," as "Melchizadec," or "The Slain Lamb," but as the "Captain of the Lord's Host." God knew that Joshua, the warrior, could not be successful until he knew his Captain. He must have a meeting with God prior to bringing down the walls of Jericho. Before Joshua could be the leader God wanted him to be, he had to have that face-to-face meeting with God.

A person planning to be a pastor must experience a meeting with the Great Shepherd. There is an agony which enters into the soul of a shepherd that comes to no other ministry. There must be times when that person comes before God, crying for God's people. The shepherd must be able to say, "God, let me die for these people. I would gladly give my life for the sheep." This is not a response from the natural man, but is one which will come from the person who has had a face-to-face confrontation with the Great Shepherd.

The person who is called to the mission field must experience a meeting with the Lord of the Harvest, for the natural man would not choose to live on the mission field with the rats, flies, dirt, and rejection which accompany this particular call of God. When the Spirit of God ministers to an individual during that time of the face-to-face meeting, God reveals Himself in a dimension which enables the fulfillment of the call of God upon that particular life. This fact is true for every person, regardless of the ministry to which he has been called.

Joshua's response to the Captain of the Lord's Host was worship. He fell on his face to the earth and worshipped, saying unto Him, "What saith my Lord unto his servant? And the captain of the LORD's host said unto Joshua, Loose thy shoe from off thy foot; for the place whereon thou standest is holy" (Josh. 5:14,15). Joshua removed his shoes as a sign that he was accepting change. From that day on, there was no resemblance between the Joshua who had ministered unto Moses and the Joshua who went through Canaan. Because Joshua responded to God during this face-to-face confrontation, he was able to take Israel into Canaan. The direction of Joshua's life changed when he became a worshipper.

Ruth

The book of Ruth is an account of Ruth, a Moabite maiden, who came into union with Boaz, the lord of the harvest. This account presents three days of choice in the life of Ruth. Associated with these three days are three levels of relationship between Boaz and Ruth. As we examine these three days in the life of Ruth, we can trace the development of her relationship with Boaz.

The first day. The "first day" in the life of Ruth began when Naomi, Ruth's mother-in-law, heard of how the Lord had visited His people and decided to return to Behlehemjudah. When Naomi suggested her daughters-in-law remain in Moab, Ruth said, "Intreat me not to leave thee, or to return from following after thee: for whither thou goest, I will go; and where thou lodgest, I will lodge: thy people shall be my people, and thy God my God: Where thou diest, will I die, and there will I be buried: the LORD do so to me, and more also, if ought but death part thee and me" (Ruth 1:16,17). At the time Ruth chose to align herself with Naomi's people, Ruth had no personal relationship with Boaz; she knew of him only as a kinsman. Because she had heard the fame of this man, she forsook her home, her people and her heathen gods in order to align herself with Bethlehemjudah and Boaz.

There is a time in our lives when each of us hears about the land of praise, and then comes a day when we must choose whether we will stay in a familiar land or move into Bethlehemjudah, that place where the Lord gives bread unto His people. At the time we choose to move into the land, we have no intimate relationship with Boaz; we have only heard the fame of the land in which he dwells. Entering into relationship with Boaz requires that we make a further choice.

The second day. When Ruth first met Boaz, she was gleaning corn in his field. She asked permission to glean among the sheaves after the reapers. When he gave permission, "Then she fell on her face, and bowed herself to the ground, and said unto him, Why have I found grace in thine eyes, that thou shouldest take knowledge of me, seeing I am a stranger?" (Ruth 2:10). This is the first mention of worship in the book of Ruth.

When we have a meeting with God, suddenly we realize what we are. When Isaiah met the Lord, he said, "Woe is me! for I am undone; because I am a man of unclean lips, and I dwell in the midst of a people of unclean lips: for mine eyes have seen the King, the LORD of hosts" (Isa. 6:5). We, too, utter this cry, saying, "Why have I found grace in Your sight? I was a heathen gentile, and You loved me before I ever loved You. Why did You love me so?" This was the cry of Ruth as she bowed herself before Boaz, the lord of the harvest.

Some people think that present day happenings on the mission fields of the world are the ultimate in God's plan for reaching the nations. However, there is more involved in the plan of God than what has already come to pass, for meeting with the Lord of the Harvest is not the final level of relationship with Jesus. Just as there was a third realm in the relationship between Ruth and Boaz, so is there a third realm of relationship between the Church and the Lord of the Harvest. This third realm of relationship and worship is entered through choice.

The third day. There came a time when Ruth neither gleaned in the harvest field nor remained with Naomi. So great was her love for Boaz and her desire for union with him, that in total submission she prostrated herself at his feet at the midnight hour. As Ruth lay at his feet Boaz said, "Who are thou?" "I am Ruth thine handmaid: spread therefore thy skirt over thine handmaid; for thou art a near kinsman" (Ruth 3:9).

With this act of total submission she risked everything she had, her home, her security, and her reputation. If she had not been accepted by Boaz, she could have been cast out and stoned as a woman of immorality. In response to Ruth's request, Boaz said, "And now, my daughter, fear not; I will do to thee all that thou requirest: for all the city of my people doth know that thou art a virtuous woman. And now it is true that I am thy near kinsman: howbeit there is a kinsman nearer than I. Tarry this night, and it shall be in the morning, that if he will perform unto thee the part of a kinsman, well; let him do the kinsman's part: but if he will not do the part of a kinsman to thee, then will I do the part of a kinsman to thee, as the LORD liveth: lie down until the morning" (Ruth 3:11-13).

When Boaz spoke to Ruth, she knew she had been accepted. She knew Boaz would pay the price necessary for her redemption. When Ruth had been fully redeemed, Boaz took her to himself. She was brought into union with the lord of the harvest. No longer was she required to glean in the field, because when she came into union with the lord of the harvest, she owned the whole harvest! It is this relationship which Paul spoke of when he said that we are heirs of God and joint heirs with Christ.

There is a higher realm of worship available to God's people than the Church has yet touched. There is a new day coming to the Church, when God will bring worshippers into union with Himself. In that third day we will risk everything we have, our homes, our security, or our reputations, in order that we might stand before Him wearing the covering of His glory. God desires a Church that has moved from praise into worship, and through worship into union with the Lord of the Harvest. The relationship of union between the Church and the Lord of the Harvest is part of the new day which God is bringing to the Church.

There will come a day when God will reveal keys to the nations of the earth. When He touches a nation, it will be open to the gospel. As each nation is touched, God will say to some of His people who are in union with the Lord of the Harvest, "I want to give you this nation. Would you take this nation for me?" These people will reply, "Yes, Lord. We want to see this nation turn to Thee." The worshipping Church which has become one with the Lord of the Harvest, will walk into the nation and take it for Jesus! As nation after nation is touched by the Spirit of God and by those who have come into union with the Lord of the Harvest, we will see the knowledge of the glory of the Lord cover the earth as the waters cover the sea. We will experience the fulfillment of the Word of the Lord, "But as truly as I live, all the earth shall be filled with the glory of the LORD" (Num. 14:21). No man will receive the glory in that mighty move of God!

Hannah

Hannah, the wife of Elkanah, was a woman of mount Ephraim who desired to have a son (1 Sam. 1:1-20). Year after year she asked the Lord to open her womb. One year as she prayed, she vowed to the Lord that if He would give her a son, she would present him unto the Lord. When the word of the Lord came to Hannah that she had received the answer to her petition, she worshipped. Although she was required to wait for a period of time for the birth of her son, Hannah waited patiently. She knew that time was required for the answer to grow before it could be presented.

Many times we petition God, touching Him for those petitions. Because we do not see the word of the Lord come to pass immediately we become unhappy. Often we begin to beg God for these previously granted petitions. First John 5:14 and 15 tells us, "And this is the confidence that we have in him, that, if we ask anything according to his will, he heareth us: And if we know that he hear us, whatsoever we ask, we know that we have the petitions that we desired of him." Once we have touched God on a subject, we should worship the Lord until we see the answer come to pass.

David

After David took Bathsheba to be his wife, Nathan the prophet was sent by God to deliver the word of the Lord to him. When David confessed to Nathan that he had sinned against the Lord, Nathan said, "The LORD also hath put away thy sin; thou shalt not die. Howbeit, because by this deed thou hast given great occasion to the enemies of the LORD to blaspheme, the child also that is born unto thee shall surely die" (2 Sam. 12:13,14). After Nathan departed, the child became ill. David sought the Lord for the child, fasting and weeping for seven days. At the end of the seven days, the child died.

David's first act following the death of his child was to arise from the earth, wash, anoint himself, change his apparel, and go to the house of the Lord (v.20). David knew that once he had confessed his sin and had received forgiveness, his rightful place was in the presence of God, worshipping. Often, after we have erred, we wear "garments of mourning," announcing to the world that we have sinned and we forget Psalms 30:11: "Thou hast turned for me my mourning into

dancing: thou has put off my sackcloth, and girded me
with gladness.'' When we insist on wearing our
"garments of mourning," we violate Romans 8:1:
"There is therefore now no condemnation to them
which are in Christ Jesus, who walk not after the flesh,
but after the Spirit.'' After we have received forgiveness for sin, our rightful position before God is that of a
priest. God loves us in spite of our imperfections, and
He desires that we worship Him.

The Congregation of Israel

At the time of David's announcement to the congregation that Solomon would build the house of the Lord,
David asked for volunteers who would consecrate their
services unto the Lord (1 Chron. 29:5). Not only did he
receive volunteers to build, but he also received
offerings of gold, silver, brass, iron, and precious
stones. He received abundant offerings for the house of
the Lord because he was willing to give freely of his
own personal treasures to the work on the temple. As
the people rejoiced, David blessed the Lord before all
the congregation, acknowledging that everything they
had given came from the hand of God. When David
finished blessing the Lord, he commanded the entire
congregation to bless the Lord. "And David said to all
the congregation, Now bless the LORD your God. And
all the congregation blessed the LORD God of their
fathers, and bowed down their heads, and worshipped
the LORD, and the king'' (v.20).

There are times when we bless the Lord because of a
personal desire to minister unto Him. Other times we
bless Him because of our desire to be obedient to His

Word. There are also times during a worship service when the ministry instructs the congregation to worship in a certain manner, just as David commanded the entire congregation to bless the Lord. At those times we please the heart of God when we respond to the direction of the worship leader. Here we see an entire congregation prostrating themselves before the Lord in obedience to the command of David the king.

Jehoshaphat

When Jehoshaphat was king of Judah, a great multitude of people came against them. When Jehoshaphat heard this news, he proclaimed a fast throughout Judah, gathered them together to ask help of the Lord. After Jehoshaphat prayed, the Spirit of the Lord came upon Jahaziel, one of the sons of Asaph. He said, "Be not afraid nor dismayed by reason of this great multitude; for the battle is not yours, but God's" (2 Chron. 20:15). The Lord then gave Judah the instructions for the battle (v.16,17). As the word of the Lord came forth, Jehoshaphat and all the inhabitants of Jerusalem and Judah fell before the Lord, worshipping Him.

Judah was in a precarious position, about to be attacked by a great multitude of warriors, there was no recourse but to rely upon the Lord. What an amazed people this must have been when the Lord said, "Stand still! You do not need to fight in this battle!" Surely some must have wondered at the word of the Lord! However, they bowed before the Lord, worshipping and acknowledging their dependance upon Him.

Second Chronicles 20:21 tells us that Jehoshaphat appointed singers to go before the army, praising the beauty of holiness. These singers were to say, "Praise the LORD; for his mercy endureth for ever." As the singers of Judah praised the Lord, He brought such confusion to their enemies, they fought against each other, destroying themselves. The fear of God came upon the surrounding countries when they heard that the Lord fought against the enemies of Israel.

In times of warfare, the Lord will often give us instructions that confound our natural minds. At those times, our best response is to fall upon our faces, worship the Lord, and acknowledge that in His hand rests our salvation. When we submit ourselves unto the Lord, we surely will see the salvation of the Lord with us!

Hezekiah

Second Chronicles 29:1 through 17 gives the account of the cleansing of the house of the Lord under the reign of Hezekiah. When the house had been cleansed, Hezekiah gathered the rulers of the city and went up to worship. Verses 21 through 24 tell of the burnt offerings which were offered for Israel, while verses 25 through 28 describe the worship which took place during the time of the burnt offering. Verse 29 tells us that when they had made an end of offering, the king and all that were present with him bowed themselves, and worshipped. As this chapter continues, we see the people consecrating themselves and bringing sacrifices and offerings of thanksgiving unto the house of the Lord (v.30,31). Verses 35 and 36 summarize the account, saying, "So the service of the house of the LORD was set in order. Hezekiah rejoiced, and all the people, that

God had prepared the people: for the thing was done suddenly".

Among the things which occurred when the service of the house of the Lord was set in order, was the bowing of the people in worship. Today God is cleansing His temple. When the cleansing has been accomplished, there will be a new consecration of God's people who will gather together, offering unto the Lord thanksgiving. At this time, the Church will not only sing praises with gladness, but will also bow in worship unto the Lord. There is coming a day to the Church in which the service of the house of the Lord will be set in order. God grant that we might be prepared for that day, entering into a celebration of worship and rejoicing before the Lord!

The Wise Men

The visit of the wise men from the east who came to worship the baby Jesus (although most Bible scholars agree that Jesus must have been about two years old at the time of their visit) seems to be shrouded in mystery. The Bible tells us very little about them. Most likely they were astrologers or learned men from the Asian culture, who spent their lives studying the heavens. When the star appeared, these men followed this strange star to its resting place. We know, of course, that they were led by the Holy Spirit. The wise men must have possessed a good knowledge of the Hebrew Scriptures, for they knew it was "he that is born King of the Jews" whom they sought. Matthew 2:2 indicates their intention was to worship this King of the Jews, heathen though they were. They brought to Him gifts of gold, frankincense, and myrrh, again confirming that the desire to worship and to sacrifice dwells deep within the heart of every man.

Today wise men still seek out the King and fall in worship before Him. Wise men still bring their treasures to pour out at His feet, and wise men still keep their eyes fixed upon the heavenlies, knowing it is again time for His star, this time THE MORNING STAR HIMSELF, to lead them to the place of His habitation!

Jesus

After Jesus was baptized in water, He was led of the Spirit into the wilderness to be tempted of the devil. Jesus' greatest area of temptation was that of worship. Satan would not have been satisfied had Jesus turned the stones into bread, neither would he have been satisfied if Jesus had cast Himself from the pinnacle of the temple. The one thing which was literally burning and eating into the mind of the Evil One, was a desire to receive the worship to which he had been exposed in the realm of the Eternals before he fell. Before Satan fell, he was "the anointed cherub that covereth" (Ezek. 28:14), he had been the guardian of God's throne, the one responsible for the atmosphere which continually surrounded the throne of God.

The devil took Jesus up into an exceeding high mountain. Showing Him all the kingdoms of this world, and the glory of them, "And saith unto him, All these things will I give thee, if thou wilt fall down and worship me" (Matt. 4:9). His greatest desire was to receive unto himself the pouring out of worship, love,

and adoration which he had witnessed in heaven
before he fell, and which the redeemed Church one
day, will pour out upon the Father! Revelation 11:15
tells us, "The kingdoms of this world are become the
kingdoms of our Lord, and of his Christ."

Jesus said, "Thou shalt worship the Lord thy God,
and him only shalt thou *serve*" (Matt. 4:10). Not only
are we to prostrate ourselves in adoration before the
Father, but we are to *serve* Him, dedicating our lives to
fulfilling His will. True worship unto the Father
involves service!

Those with Needs

Several examples of worship given in the book of
Matthew demonstrate the importance of worship in
the prayer life of the believer. Matthew 8:1 and 2:
"When he was come down from the mountain, great
multitudes followed him. And, behold, there came a
leper and worshipped him, saying, Lord, if thou wilt,
thou canst make me clean." Matthew 9:18: "While he
spake these things unto them, behold, there came a
certain ruler, and worshipped him, saying, My daughter
is even now dead: but come and lay thy hand upon her,
and she shall live." Matthew 15:22 and 25: "And, behold,
a woman of Canaan came out of the same coasts, and
cried unto him, saying, Have mercy on me, O Lord,
thou Son of David; my daughter is grievously vexed
with a devil... Then came she and worshipped him,
saying, Lord, help me." Matthew 18:26: "The servant
therefore fell down, and worshipped him, saying, Lord,
have patience with me, and I will pay thee all." Finally,
Matthew 20:20: "Then came to him the mother of

Zebedee's children with her sons, worshipping him, and desiring a certain thing of him."

There is a thread running through each of these Scriptures. Each individual had a problem, and each one presented that need to Jesus in an atmosphere of worship. In each of these circumstances, Jesus answered prayer, worked miracles, and gave to the worshippers the desires of their hearts. There is no doubt that in many of these cases (or perhaps in all) the depth of worship was shallow; however, the examples reveal a truth which many of us miss. We spend much of our prayer time begging God for answers to our most pressing needs, trying to exercise faith to believe that the answer is on the way. Very few times do we engage ourselves in just pouring out at His feet our love and adoration, regardless of how pressing or how urgent may be our need. There is a very vital area of warfare in the realm of worship, but it is good to know that bowing at His feet and loving Him produces an atmosphere in which prayer is answered and miracles occur! Have we, as God's people missed this realm through the years? Have we missed this realm by always coming before God with our requests and not with our worship?

Disciples

When the disciples met Jesus after His resurrection, they fell down at His feet and worshipped Him (Matt. 28:9). What a beautiful picture of worship that was! The Bible also tells us that some doubted (Matt. 28:16,17). Not everyone who hears the message of worship will pay the price required to become a worshipper. Some will say, "I do not know if this is the answer." Others will pay the price. They will fall before God in worship because they count Him to be more worthy than houses, lands, fortune, ministry, or acclaim. They know that everything God is doing in the earth today, along with everything we individually experience in God, springs from the womb of worship. They know that every problem we have can be answered if we would become worshippers, true worshippers of the Lamb.

The Woman at the Well

John 4:1-30 gives the account of the woman at the well. While Jesus was at Jacob's well, a Samaritan woman came to draw water, and as they engaged in conversation, Jesus asked this woman to call her husband. When she replied that she had no husband, Jesus said, "Thou hast well said, I have no husband...For thou hast had five husbands; and he whom thou now hast is not thy husband: in that saidst thou truly" (v.17,18).

Many people have criticized this woman for "living in sin." However, Jesus did not criticize her. In fact, He never again mentioned her immorality. He knew the need of the Samaritan woman did not involve her immoral living, it was worship. Jesus cast *no* "unclean devils" out of this woman. The reason she had been driven to immorality, and was unable to be satisfied, was because she had not learned worship. Many times we criticize the actions of people without realizing that those actions are the symptoms of a seeking heart. Failing to acknowledge that moral problems are not a

cause, but a symptom of a deeper need, we demand that
the offensive behavior change, only to find another
offensive behavior developing in its place. The fullness
of worship touches deeply the matter of deliverance
and involves not only deliverance *from* bondages, but
also deliverance *unto* Him. Only a full and lasting love
relationship with the Lord Jesus can bring about the
lasting changes we so long for!

As the Spirit of God opened this woman's heart by a
word of knowledge, she recognized she was in the
presence of One Who could answer her deepest need.
Her immediate response was, "Oh, I see that you are a
prophet. Will you tell me about worship? Our fathers
worshipped in this mountain; but you say that Jerusalem is the place where men ought to worship." In
answer to her question, Jesus said, in essence, "Woman,
your perspective is very narrow right now. All you
know is that there is a controversy between whether
you are to worship here on this mountain or at
Jerusalem. I don't even want to enter into that controversy. You do not know what you are worshipping,
for salvation is of the Jews! But the hour cometh, and
now is, when the true worshippers shall worship the
Father in spirit and in truth: *for the Father seeketh
such to worship Him.*"

There is a fine, delicate, yet secure balance between
Spirit (the anointing) and truth (The Word of God).
Without this balance we make room for error. Some
people have emphasized the moving of the Spirit of
God, but they have neglected truth. Others have
emphasized truth without the anointing. Today, the
Church is striving to achieve the balance between

Spirit and truth which the word of God says will produce true worshippers. True worshippers are those who bring truths of the Word of God under the canopy of the anointing, thereby achieving the delicate balance between Spirit and truth, which brings them into acceptable worship before God. True worship never violates the Word of God.

As the Church comes into more and more understanding of the expression of worship, there must also come equal understanding of truth. Our understanding of the Word should be continually expanding in order that every expression of our worship might flow safely within the perimeter of God's Word. In the past, when the Spirit of God has moved, denominations have set up walls around the portions of truth which were revealed. When men camped around these, making for themselves secure dwelling places, the balance between Spirit and truth was eventually lost. Every fresh sweep of the Spirit of God is dissipated when men put a period behind whatever God is currently doing and refuse to accept further change. Today there is a great cry in the heart of God for men to worship Him. The Father is still seeking true worshippers, those who will become vehicles of expression which will satisfy His heart. As we develop our individual relationships with the Father, the cry of each of our hearts should be, "Father, will You continually change me? I want to be a true worshipper. I want to worship You in Spirit and in Truth (in the Spirit and according to the Word)."

The Angels

Although man was created a little lower than the angels (Ps. 8:5), angels are never elevated above the

Son of God. The angels do not know God as their Father; they do not possess that Name which is above all other names. At the birth of Jesus, Who was to have that More Excellent Name, the Father issued a command, "Let all the angels of God worship him" (Heb. 1:6). At that time the heavens were rent and the angels of heaven bowed low, pouring out their adoration upon the Lord, "Glory to God in the highest, and on earth peace, good will toward men" (Luke 2:14).

Through redemption man has been elevated to a position higher than angels and has been given songs of worship which the angels cannot sing. Revelation 5:9 and 10 states, "And they sang a new song" and Revelation 15:3 and 4 speaks of "the song of Moses...and the song of the Lamb." The song of Moses, a song of deliverance, is found in Exodus 15:1 through 21. "I will sing unto the LORD, for he hath triumphed gloriously: the horse and his rider hath he thrown into the sea." Throughout eternity God's people will sing this great song of deliverance, telling how God has redeemed them from the hand of the enemy.

The song of the Lamb is the song of worship which is now being added to the Church. For years we have heard the song of Moses (song of deliverance), but ascending now unto the heavenlies is the voice of the redeemed Church, singing, "Thou art worthy, O Lord" (Rev. 4:11). "Thou Art Worthy" is the song of the worshippers of the Lamb, who have so fallen in love with Him they will follow Him whithersoever He goeth, knowing that for His pleasure they were created!

Jacob

When Jacob knew it was time to die, he did not say,

"On, no! I am going to die!" Death to him was no enemy. He said, "Come, my sons. I have something to do. I shall lay hands on you and prophesy over you, and what I prophesy will come to pass." Then he *worshipped*, leaning on his staff (Heb. 11:21).

In the course of many years of ministry, I have had opportunity to be with people as they have entered eternity. I have seen both Christians and unsaved men die. One of the greatest blessings a human life can experience is that moment when eternity touches time, and God claims one of His own. That moment is the most triumphant moment in the life of a worshipper. Regardless of how we enter eternity, whether through physical death or one day through the translation, the greatest moment of our lives is when, on the wings of worship, we are ushered into the presence of the Lord Jesus. There is something sacred about death when one of God's children goes into the presence of the Lord in an atmosphere of worship.

What a mantle must have rested on this great patriarch, Jacob, when in his dying moments he could gather together his sons and prophesy over each one words of truth which are still being fulfilled, and then without fear or struggle be gathered to his fathers, as the Word says. God grant the Church today such victory over death and such a mantle of anointing right to the end!

The Four and Twenty Elders

What is the purpose of your life? Were you born to be a singer? Were you born to be a teacher? Were you born to be a missionary? You were not born to be any of these, you were born to be a WORSHIPPER! The realm of worship into which God is bringing the Church is far beyond *our* ministries, *our* desires, or "doing our thing," going here and there. God wants to bring His people to the place where they will do only that which brings pleasure unto Him. Ministry is always secondary to worship. True ministry becomes only one of the many expressions of worship.

Revelation 14:4 declares, "These are they which follow the Lamb whithersoever He goeth." Those who follow the Lamb whithersoever He goes, cannot have any ties to this earth that will weaken their love for Jesus and their commitment to His will. Earthly ties must not weaken their commitment to their first love. When the Lamb moves, "they which follow the Lamb" must move with Him. There will be a company of people in the last-day Church who will follow the Lamb whithersoever He goeth. In these last glorious days of the Church, our motivation for ministry will completely change. Desire for success and the acclaim of men will be replaced by a burning passion to bring pleasure unto Him, whom we adore, and for whose pleasure we were created.

Revelation 5:11 through 14, 7:9 through 12 and 11:16 and 17, present accounts of worshippers before the throne of God. The elders, the four beasts, the angels, the twenty-four elders, prostrate themselves before God, offering thanksgiving, praise, and adoration unto Him that liveth for ever and ever.

The Worshippers

A spiritual commission is being issued to the Church

today: "Rise, and measure the temple of God, and the altar, and them that worship therein" (Rev. 11:1).

The temple of God is to be measured. The Bible tells us our bodies are the temple of the Holy Ghost. Today God is measuring what we are doing with the temple of the Holy Ghost.

The altar is to be measured. Our altars must be built upon foundations which will support the exceeding weight of glory that God desires to place upon His Church. Worship strengthens the altars of our lives.

The worshippers are to be measured. God the Father is looking for true worshippers. He is not looking for those who "worship" only on Sunday morning (if this could be possible for a true worshipper), but for those whose entire lives are expressions of worship unto Him. He is looking for those to whom worship is a life, preparing them to bring pleasure unto Him throughout eternity. Today God is saying, "Take the rod and measure the people. See how far they have grown unto the measure of the stature of the fulness of Christ." God does not demand from a spiritual babe what He demands from a mature Christian. However, He does require growth from each of His people. God wants us to grow so that we might measure up to His standards. He wants us to develop according to His Word.

Worship Before the Throne of God

Revelation 19 presents an account of a great volume of worship being offered to God for His true and righteous judgments. When I read this chapter, I realize how vast will be the multitudes of those who will praise and worship the Lord throughout eternity, and "I bow my knees unto the Father of our Lord Jesus Christ, Of whom *the whole family in heaven and earth* is named" (Eph. 3:14,15). As the four and twenty elders and the four beasts fell down and worshipped God, a command was given: "Praise our God, all ye his servants, and ye that fear him, both small and great" (Rev. 19:5). This command was spoken not only to the ministry and to the "spiritual", but it was spoken to *all* of His servants and to *all* that fear God, both small and great. Therefore, if you are a servant of God and if you fear Him, then you are expected to praise the Lord.

There will come a day when the multitudes will surround the throne of God, praising Him for His merciful judgments, and there will be "the voice of a great multitude, and as the voice of many waters, and as the voice of mighty thunderings, saying, Alleluia: for the Lord God omnipotent reigneth. Let us be glad and rejoice, and give honour to him: the marriage of the Lamb is come, and his wife hath made herself ready" (v.6,7). Worship is not a profitless activity, but it will prepare us for the marriage supper of the Lamb, the time when we will enter into union with The Lord Jesus Christ.

John the Revelator

Revelation 22:8 and 9 presents the last reference to worship in the New Testament. It is interesting to note that this last biblical reference to worship involves an admonition to worship God, rather than one of His servants. John received this admonition at a time when he had experienced spiritual revelation. Despite the level of his spiritual experience, John fell prey to an error common to many of God's people; he prostrated himself in worship before someone who was more spiritually mature than he. Regardless of where we are in our walk with God, regardless of how far we have developed into the fulness of the measure of the stature of Christ, we need to guard against worshipping any person other than the Lord. It is noteworthy that this angel at whose feet John fell immediately corrected the situation, saying, "See thou do it not: for I am thy fellow servant...and of them which keep the sayings of this book: worship God" (v.9). Individuals who have walked with God have a responsibility to those who are younger in the Lord. The eyes of the younger Christian should be turned toward the Lamb of God, for unto Him belongs all blessing, glory, wisdom, thanksgiving, honor, power, and might. Those who follow the Lamb whithersoever He goeth, must also direct others to follow the Lamb and to worship God.

Kneeling in Worship

Kneeling is a bodily position commonly used in prayer. The Scripture tells us that when Jesus was on the mount of Olives, He knelt down and prayed (Luke 22:41). As Stephen was being stoned, he knelt down and cried out to God (Acts 7:59,60). At the bedside of Dorcas, Peter knelt down and prayed, asking God to raise her from the dead (Acts 9:40). When Paul wrote to the Church in Ephesus, he said, "For this cause I bow my knees unto the Father of our Lord Jesus Christ, of whom the whole family in heaven and earth is named" (Eph. 3:14,15). Kneeling is not exclusively used for prayer, for David said, "O come, let us worship and bow down: let us kneel before the LORD our maker. For he is our God; and we are the people of his pasture, and the sheep of his hand" (Ps. 95:6,7). Romans 14:11 tells us that every knee shall bow and every tongue shall confess to God. Phillipians 2:10 and 11 declares that at the Name of Jesus every knee shall bow and every tongue confess that Jesus Christ is Lord. There is a time when we use the form of kneeling in our corporate worship; as a congregation we kneel before the Lord, acknowledging that we are His people and the sheep of His pasture. As we kneel before the Lord, we not only receive the blessing of His presence, but we are bowing in the humility of worship before Him.

Throughout eternity a people will be gathered about the throne of God, bowing before Him, blessing His Name, and declaring: "Blessing, and honour, and glory, and power, be unto him that sitteth upon the throne, and unto the Lamb for ever and ever" (Rev. 5:13). Heaven will be filled with worship!

Chapter Six

Role of Music in the Church

Instruments of Music

Unto Adam was born Cain, unto Cain was born Enoch, unto Enoch was born Lamech, and in the eighth generation from Adam through the lineage of Cain, was born Jubal. "He was the father of all such as handle the harp and organ" (Gen. 4:21). "Jubal" is the Hebrew word meaning "stream, or to flow," and is similar to the word "Jubilee" meaning "blast of a horn" (from its continuous or streaming sound). Both words are from a Hebrew root word meaning "to flow or bring, especially with pomp, to carry or lead forth." Certainly music flows forth from musical instruments and has the ability to carry or lead forth. Even a staccato must "carry onward," having a flowing sound which can carry on like a river or stream. Most interesting is the fact that the word "Jubilee" is used by God to describe a great celebration occurring every fifty years on the day of atonement, designating the great release of His people from bondage, debt, and slavery. To signal the release, the horn of Jubilee was to sound loud and long.

It is also interesting to note that to the seed of Cain (who, no doubt, were heavily oppressed as a result of the wickedness and rebellion so obvious in their fathers) God gave the expression of music, that their soul might know a lifting and release. How merciful is God Who sends His refreshing rain on the just and the unjust alike.

God, Himself, is the originator of song and musical instruments. Melody and harmony have their source in Him. Long before the creation of this earth, God created morning stars whose singing we can only try to imagine. In Job 38:7, we find that they were singing while God was creating the earth. Oh, what a wonder that the very formation and balancing of our earth was accomplished to the melody of the morning stars and the shouts of the sons of God. How unsearchable are His judgments and His ways past finding out!

When, David, the sweet psalmist of Israel was king, the melody of heaven grew so strong within him that he found the musical instruments of his day were inadequate to manifest the sounds that were in his heart. So by the inspiration of God, King David designed and made musical instruments for the sole purpose of worshipping God (2 Chron. 7:6; Neh. 12:36). There is no doubt that he received the design of these instruments by inspiration, for we are told that he was given specific instructions for the service of the house of God including the worship, courses, and activity in every area. The complete pattern was shown to him. God promised to give to him willing and skillful workmen, who could perform any manner of service for the house of God.

Eventually, God also showed other servants the worship of heaven, and instructed them to write it down that we might have it today. In the book of Revelation, John must have been shown: worshippers who have the harps of God (Rev. 15:2), harpers harping with their harps and singing (Rev. 14:2,3), and the twenty-four elders and four beasts having every one of them harps and singing (Rev. 5:8,9).

Musical instruments have no ability of themselves to convey life-giving sound. Their effectiveness depends entirely upon the skill of the craftsmen who fashion them and the musicians who handle them. The musician must be aware that within *all* humanity is musical receptivity and response, but musicians and singers have a special ability to formulate and communicate their message through music. We are all created in the image and likeness of the Chief Musician and Master Singer, the Creator of melody, voice, and sound but God has given particular ability to some in this area. Every musician shall give account to God for the use or misuse of this talent.

By the ministry of music, demons are forced to retreat (1 Sam. 16:16,23). By the ministry of music, the Spirit of God in revelation, wisdom, and knowledge is released (2 Kings 3:14-19). By the ministry of music, enemies are defeated (2 Chron. 20:14-30). God's power and creative ability are released, and cooperate with the pure music of the minstrel. The earth and all that is in it was fashioned, established, balanced, measured and fastened to the accompaniment of music.

Minstrels can allow God to control them and flow freely through them so they might be used as He intended, or they can allow their own fleshly desires to direct them. They can even allow the devil to benefit from their ministry. Consider this account in Isaiah 5:11 and 12 (AMP), "Woe unto those who rise early in the morning that they may pursue strong drink, who tarry late into the night till wine inflames them. They have the lyre, and harp, tambourine and flute and wine at their feast but they do not regard the deeds of the Lord, neither consider the operation of His hands in mercy and judgment." *This music is used entirely for sensual pleasure.*

Consider also Daniel 3:5, "That at what time ye hear the sound of the cornet, flute, harp, sackbut, psaltery, dulcimer, and all kinds of musick, ye fall down and worship the golden image that Nebuchadnezzar the king hath set up." This music is used for the purpose of the devil, to cause people to bow down to him instead of to God.

Today there is a great surge of sinful music in the world. He who has heard the music which surrounds the throne of God, knows that the fulness of the music of heaven will soon be restored to the Church. The devil's influence upon the music of the world during this present age, is an attempt to provide a distracting counterfeit to the music which will be made manifest in the last-day Church.

When we understand that music, with its variety of instruments, songs, chants, and rhythms, and its vast scope from simple tune to regal orchestration, has its origin within the heart of the Eternal God, can we be content with that which flesh has produced, though it be counted as excellent? Or can we agree with music stained with the demonic? As we are awakened more and more to that which heaven hears, and which we were created to know and to express, shall we not earnestly desire that the music of heaven, the eternal song, fill all the earth also?

Psalms, Hymns and Spiritual Songs

Singing songs in church is not only an effective means of expressing praise and worship to God, but also is a means of teaching, admonishing, exhorting, and edifying one another and ourselves (Col. 3:16; Eph. 5:19). Singing is a ministry to God and to His people that every believer is urged to exercise. The song may take the form of a very simple lyric expressing feelings of praise and thanksgiving to God; it may be an anthem of worship which others can learn and sing also; or it may be a prophetic song through which God speaks to His people. Music and song should include both the expression of the believer and the expression of the mind and heart of God.

One of the books of the Bible bears the title "The Song of Solomon," and the first verse defines the book as "the song of songs." Just as Jesus is declared to be King of kings, so is this book declared to be the Song of Songs — the example, the utmost, the most excellent, the supreme song. We learn from this beautiful book that as God is singing to us, He builds us while speaking edifying, creative words. He teaches us, not by saying how weak and unbecoming we are, but by how beautiful and strong. The song *changes* us; it changes our attitudes about ourselves and others, and draws us into a relationship of love with Him.

Therefore, we understand that *song* has the ability to change attitudes and emotions. It has the ability to shape and mold thoughts and concepts. The Song of Songs serves as an example to us, revealing the heart of the Bridegroom and the Bride. When such songs are sung spontaneously in the congregation of believers, they become a beautiful vehicle of worship and praise. The Song of Songs is an expression of God's creative love for His people and the response of the Church to Him.

There is also what may be called "harvest singing." The songs of joy and victory, power and deliverance, and thanksgiving for the bountiful blessings and abundant life which we have received from God. Harvest singing is a *response*; it is spontaneous singing by members of the Body of Christ, often climaxing in joyous dancing and celebration of the greatness of our God. The songs should carry the same theme and tune, usually having one master singer who carries the theme to which others respond after each stanza. Example:

Master singer:
    Who is He that giveth victory
    That only doeth wondrous things
    That setteth all the captives free.
    That loosed the chains which held men bound,
    And broke the power of the enemy.
    What is His name and who is He?
Responsive Singer:
    He is the King of Glory.

He is the Son of God.
His is our Saviour Jesus.
He is Emmanuel.
He heals the brokenhearted,
He liberates the bruised.
He gives sight to the blind,
Strength to the lame,
And none will He refuse.

The song may continue as the singers magnify God and declare His wondrous works. This type of song may also be seen in Exodus 15:1 through 21. Moses was the master singer and the congregation responded with verse 21 (probably intermittently throughout the song). Led by Miriam, they danced joyously with timbrels. Many of the Psalms were sung in this manner, especially Psalms 113 through 118. Harvest singing is also seen in Ezra 3:10 and 11 and Nehemiah 12:27 and 40. This type of song is often accompanied by joyous shouting (Isa. 61:10; Jer. 48:33; Num. 23:21; Ps. 47:5; Ps. 132:9).

Another type of singing is the *prophetic song*. The message of the song may be couched between praises of the Lord and declaration of His greatness, but the impact and intent of the song is a prophetic message from God to His people. An example of this is the song which God gave Moses to sing to the people. He told Moses to teach the people to sing it also. "Now therefore write ye this song for you, and teach it to the children of Israel: put it in their mouths...And Moses spake in the ears of all the congregation of Israel the words of this song, until they were ended" (Deut. 31:19,30). The song God gave to Moses is found in Deuteronomy 32:1 through 43.

In the prophetic song, the prophet is totally identified with God; sometimes he speaks in *behalf* of God and sometimes God speaks in the first person through the prophet. The song is given by revelation, by inspiration from God. It gives a revelation of ancient days, of things present and of things to come. It declares the purposes of God, His warnings, exhortation to the people, and His promises of blessing. The prophetic song expresses the mind and heart of God. It is a beautiful expression and revelation of our King. While it is full of substance (even *heavy*, as we would say), yet it is a *song* that is very poetic, sensitive, and rhythmic. This type of singing is very majestic, very high, yet extremely clear. Nothing is vague or veiled, although poetic phrases are used.

The prophetic song is not always spontaneous. Notice that God *taught* Moses this song. He told Moses to write it down, learn it and teach it. So it is today, God teaches songs to individuals so they can be sung to the edification of the Body and to the glory of God.

Three types of songs are mentioned which are to be sung: the psalms, the hymns, and the spiritual songs. These may be defined in the following manner:

Psalms: "To celebrate the divine in song or music, to worship with prayer or praise set to music." The psalm is written to magnify the Lord, but also may give expression to that which is within (whether praise *or distress*) by song *to the Lord.* Even though the song expresses fear or distress, the Spirit of God will respond to the singer and will *always* build him up again with hope. As he sings to the Lord, God *responds* by song within the singer, edifying him. For example, in Psalms

42 there is a rhythmic movement from distress to praise, or from despair to hope. It is an intense portrayal of the troubled soul drawing life, strength, hope, and help from God.

Hymns: "A religious ode." Many Christian songs are recorded and sung by multitudes of people. Often these are called hymns. We see in Deuteronomy 32 that God, at times, specifically inspired songs and intended that they become more than a temporary blessing. They were to be recorded and taught by one generation to the next. The song which Moses taught Israel is what we would call a hymn or anthem. In it, God declares His own nature and the nature of man. He told Moses that the song was to be a witness for Himself for generations to come (Deut. 31:19,21). We have such songs in the Church now, though perhaps not involving the scope of this song; for example, "Rock of Ages," "Amazing Grace," "The Old Rugged Cross," and many more of the old enduring hymns of the Church. These songs declare the goodness, grace, and judgments of our God. They relate *eternal truth*, and they are intended to reach and teach *all* people. They possess a certain authority which other songs, though beautiful and true, do not contain. Indeed, hymns seem to convey the *official* song message of the Church, while psalms (the celebrating of God in song) involve more the song of the individual believer.

Spiritual Songs: "A supernatural or regenerate song." First Corinthians 14:15 gives instruction concerning the spiritual or supernatural song. "I will sing with the spirit, and I will sing with the understanding also." Often, a believer will find it easier to sing in

tongues because he does not have to worry about
rhyme, rhythm, or the right words to express deep
feelings. Praise and worship will well up in a beautiful
song in the Spirit, though the understanding of the
singer is unfruitful. However, the spiritual song, the
song of the Lord, must be understood to be effective.
Psalms 42:8 "in the night his song shall be with me,"
and Psalms 32:7, "thou shall compass me about with
songs of deliverance."

These songs must not be limited to the private
devotions of the believer, but should be sung in the
congregation also. Jesus said, "I will declare thy name
unto my brethren, in the midst of the church will I sing
praise unto thee" (Heb. 2:12). The spiritual song is both
the expression of humanity toward God and the expression of God toward man; the chief singer revealing the
heart of God toward His beloved Church — singing
praise and declaring His Name through yielded vessels.

Music

Psalms 149 and 150 specify that the children of Israel
used many instruments in worship: timbrels, harps,
psalteries, stringed instruments, organs and cymbals.
Today there are those who would remove from the
Church the playing of instruments, but this is far from
scriptural. As the Church increases in glory, there will
be more singing and more instrumental music than
ever before. There will not be the element of entertainment through natural talent, for there is a higher
purpose in music and song than mere entertainment.
Music is a vehicle through which God will express
Himself to the Church, and through which the Church

will express herself to God and to His people. The music of the last-day Church will ascend as a cloud of worship and blend with everything God is doing in a worship service. It is a wonderful blessing to find a pianist or organist who will abandon his or her talent unto God, and play anthems of praise under the anointing, while the congregation listens in quiet worship. There have been occasions when a pianist or organist has led an anthem of worship; as the playing progressed every instrument began to play under the same anointing, not following a musical score but playing spontaneously and forming an anthem of orchestral praise unto the Lord. With such worship heaven must be filled!

Psalms 33:3 instructs God's people to play skillfully. There is no premium on ignorance in the Kingdom of God. Natural training in the playing of an instrument is a great asset in spiritual worship. This is demonstrated in First Samuel 16:17, where Saul asked for a minstrel. As David played skillfully upon the harp under the anointing, the evil spirit was driven from Saul.

One thing God requires of His people is that they come before His presence with singing (Ps. 100:2). A large number of attending church members, do not know the true function of singing in a worship service or why they sing in church. They only know that singing is incorporated into most worship services. Singing was such an important part of the worship in the house of God, that David systematically appointed those who were to minister in music and in song. A distinct charge was laid upon them for this ministry (1 Chron. 9:33). Today, there are those in the house of God whose ministry is to enter into spiritual song during times of worship.

Nehemiah 13:5 notes that the portion to the singers was given along with the portion to the priests. Today the ministry of song is a priestly ministry, and plays an essential part in our worship. We need a new song each day as we come into the presence of the Lord (Ps. 98:1); a song which has never been sung before, a fresh response to the Lord. That new song brings refreshing to us, builds and draws us closer to Him. At a time when Israel needed water the people sang to the well, "Spring up, O well." At times we should sing to the well with our hearts. During dry seasons we can sing to that well, and the song of the Lord and the Word of God will begin to flow, watering our desert lands.

Hezekiah said, "Therefore we will sing *MY* songs to the stringed instruments all the days of our life in the house of the LORD" (Isa. 38:20). When Hezekiah realized that God had healed him and extended his life, he wrote songs and commanded they be sung in the house of God.

We are told that the singers and the porters were mentioned together. There are those in the church who have the ability to enter into the anointing. Together wth the singers, they open the door for others to enter into the presence of God. In First Chronicles 16:42 and 43, we again see the porters mentioned with those who were involved in the ministry of music.

Psalms 33:3 instructs God's people to play skillfully with a loud noise. Second Chronicles 30:21 tells us, the Levites and the priests praised the Lord day by day, singing with loud instruments unto Him. Worship in the tabernacle must have been very noisy. There must have been times of excitement as God moved upon the singers and the players of instruments. It is the responsibility of those involved in the music ministry to sing and play with all their might.

In Second Kings 3:15 Elisha called for a minstrel. When the minstrel played, the hand of the Lord came upon Elisha and he prophesied the word of the Lord. The anointing upon Elisha was dependent upon the anointing which rested upon and was released by the minstrel. Prophecy is again mentioned in connection with music in First Chronicles 25:1. This verse mentions those who prophesy with harps. As the minstrels played their harps, the spirit of prophecy would come upon them and they would prophesy. Here we see that the ministry of music involves more than entertainment. Those who are minstrels in the house of God must be open to hear the word of the Lord and to reveal His word unto the congregation.

It is interesting to note that both men and women are to sing. Ecclesiastes 2:8 tells us that Solomon gathered men singers and women singers. Ezra 2:65 and Nehemiah 7:67 both mention the presence of singing men and singing women within the congregation of Israel during the time of restoration. From these Scriptures we see that God took the trouble to mention that singing was not only for the women, but also was for the men. In David's tabernacle the singers mentioned as being set aside to a ministry were men singers (1 Chron. 15:16,19).

Those who are singers in the house of the Lord will be involved in spiritual warfare. Acts 16:25 tells us when Paul and Silas were held captive they prayed and sang praises unto God. As they ministered to the Lord, He sent an earthquake and delivered them from bondage. Today when we are held captive in negative circumstances, we can pray and sing unto the Lord, and He will set us free. Another example of the ministry of song in spiritual warfare is found in Second Chronicles 20:21. Jehoshaphat appointed singers unto the Lord to praise the beauty of holiness. As the children of Israel went into battle, the singers went before the army, saying, "Praise the Lord; for his mercy endureth forever." As they sang and praised God, He set ambushments against the enemy. God will do the same for the Church today. When there is a time of warfare, the singers should begin to sing. God will send ambushments against the enemy, breaking the yoke by His anointing.

One sign of judgment upon Israel was the lack of joy and singing (Isa. 16:9,10; Jer. 48:33). As God restored His people, singing was restored to the Church. Today harvest singing has been restored to the Church, and the noise of vintage shouting is again heard in the land.

Second Samual 19:35 speaks of Barzillai, a man who was eighty years old. Barzillai described himself as not being able to hear the voice of singing men and singing women. When a person is nearly dead, he cannot even *hear* the song of the Lord. It is no small wonder that some people cannot understand why there is so much music and singing in the Church today: they are nearly dead spiritually, they cannot even *hear* the song of the Lord.

When the true song of the Lord is missing, men will invent for themselves instruments of music *like* David (Amos 6:5). There is always a counterfeit for the real thing: when the glory departs, men must produce something *like* the anointing in an attempt to satisfy the hunger for song in the hearts of men.

First Chronicles 15:27 through 29 notes that there is a judgment which comes upon those who despise the anointing; blessings come upon those who receive and appreciate it. The spirit of Michal is still in the Church today, but those who are clothed with the garments of priesthood, will sing and rejoice in the Lord as the Ark of His presence is being restored to the Church.

Isaiah 14:7 speaks of a day when God's creation will be at rest, there will be no judgment upon the land. In that day, they will break forth into singing. Song is a sign of the rest of God, and there is a rest which comes from releasing the song of the Lord which is within.

Second Chronicles 5:13 describes the worship which filled the house of the Lord at the dedication of Solomon's temple. This account tells us that the singers and the trumpeters were as one, making one sound in praising and thanking the Lord. As the worshippers were united, the house was filled with the cloud of God's glory. Here is a pattern for the last-day Church. As we worship God in unity, the house will be filled with the presence of God.

Psalms 87:2 and 3 speak of Zion, saying, "The LORD

loveth the gates of Zion more than all the dwellings of Jacob. Glorious things are spoken of thee, O city of God.'' Why does the Lord love Zion? One reason is given in verse 7: "As well the singers as the players on instruments shall be there: all my springs are in thee.'' Verse 7 has also been translated in the following manner: "Singers and dancers alike all chant your praises, proclaiming glorious things of you, O city of God'' (NEB). What a glorious city Zion will be. Zion will be filled with music as singers, dancers, and players on instruments offer to God anthems of praise and worship, expressing the melodies of the music of heaven.

For this chapter, "The Role of Music in the Church,'' I am indebted to Gail Tait, a dear friend and anointed teacher of the Word, who moves under a mantle of revelation.

Chapter Seven

"Let Them Praise His Name In the Dance"

During times of restoration, God has added many truths to the Church, including clapping hands, praise and worship, the song of the Lord, and speaking with other tongues. Today, God is moving again, and a new kind of worship is being birthed in the Church...the expression of spiritual dancing.

One has only to read history to discover that dancing in its many forms was part of the worship of God's people. It is my opinion that dancing has its origin in praise and worship. Through the centuries this form of worship has been corrupted to the point that the Church has almost completely rejected it, rather than be associated with something so heathenish, lustful and sinful, as the dancing of the world.

Unger's Bible Dictionary tells us concerning spiritual dancing:

"A form of religious dancing sometimes made part of the public worship of the early Christians. The custom was borrowed from the Jews, in whose solemn processions choirs of young men and maidens, moving in time with solemn music, always bore a part. It must not be supposed that the "religious dances" had any similarity to modern amusements. They were rather processions, in which all who took part marched in time with the hymns which they sang. The custom was very early laid aside, probably because it might have led to the adoption of such objectionable dances as were employed in honor of the pagan deities. Prohibitions of dancing as an amusement abound in the Church fathers and in the decrees of the council."

Although dancing is perhaps the most controversial form of worship in the Christian world today, we must recognize that in the message of restoration, God promises to restore the dance to the last-day Church. Jeremiah 31:12 and 13 declares, "Therefore they shall come and sing in the height of Zion, and shall flow together to the goodness of the LORD, for wheat, and for wine, and for oil, and for the young of the flock and of the herd: and their soul shall be as a watered garden; and they shall not sorrow any more at all. *Then shall the virgin rejoice in the dance, both young men and old together: for I will turn their mourning into joy, and will comfort them, and make them rejoice from their sorrow.*"

Dancing is not new to the Christian who is familiar with worship in the realm of pentecostal churches. Since the outpouring of the Holy Spirit at the turn of the century *dancing in the Spirit* has been a part of pentecostal praise and worship. It must be noted, however, "dancing in the Spirit," the term which has been so widely used throughout the years, is not found in God's Word. Careful study of the Word reveals that the appropriate expression is *dancing before the Lord.* For example, David danced before the Lord with all his might at the time of the return of the Ark of the Covenant to Israel. "Dancing in the Spirit" suggests that the Holy Spirit takes hold of the Christian, causing him or her to enter into uncontrollable motions and contortions, all supposedly manifestations of the Spirit. "Dancing before the Lord" suggests the worshipper's strength, training, and expertise as fully under the control of the dancer, who expresses worship and joy in actions and steps which bring pleasure to the heart of God. While it is true that the believer is admonished to "leap for joy," it is also true that there are many Scriptures which indicate that intricate steps, marches, group dances, twirling, and twisting were part of the expression of the dance.

There is a growing conviction among the people of God that He is most pleased when we offer to Him, as an act of worship, all of our ability whether it be in art, in the dance, or in any other creative expression with which the Lord has blessed us. *Every* activity of life is designed to become an act of worship. In the past five years we have seen many gifted dancers come to Jesus for salvation and add to the Body of Christ a wonderful ability to express in an excellent manner, their worship unto Him in the dance. Just as there are those who have been given the ability to sing and to edify the Body through excellence in song, so are there those who have been given the ability to pour out to God a similar ministry through the dance. Room should be made within the worship structure of the Church for the full expression of each individual; such expression should always remain within the confines of the Word and under the leadership of the ministries.

As you study the Scriptures on dancing, you will notice that certain physical expressions are definitely mentioned: twirling, leaping, twisting, dancing with a measured step, dancing in chorus, and marching in regal procession. No room has been left for expression of the degraded, lustful, disgusting type of dancing, in which this world is engaged. God is very explicit about the things which please His heart. His word gives specific instructions on the subject of the dance.

To some people the words "jump" and "dance" are almost synonymous; this is not true. Although at this point the concept of expressive dancing is controversial, and sometimes is received in a negative manner when first witnessed, the openhearted, searching believer, will find a real blessing in the free (yet very controlled) expression of the dance in worship. Many people who have been given ability by God to express in the dance, have experienced a fulfillment in their personal relationship with Jesus as they began to move into worship in this manner. In dancing before the Lord and pouring out oneself through the dance, the worshipper finds great release and joy, and the total expression of the local church is enriched.

Spiritual Dancing in the Old Testament

When Israel passed over the Red Sea, there was

great rejoicing in the camp. The Lord had set His people free from the yoke of the oppressor. At this time Miriam *led* the women of Israel in a dance. Indeed, without the wisdom of Godly leadership, the truth cannot be administrated appropriately; inadequate leadership can bring reproach upon the people of God. Today God is setting His people free from bondage. He has provided strong anointed leadership to administrate the joy and rejoicing expressed by His people during times of congregational worship. The fact that most dancing recorded in Scripture was done in chorus, indicates God's highest order in the dance is for the entire church to move into the dance *together*.

Judges 11:34 presents the account of Jephthah returning from battle. When Jephthah came to his house, his daughter came to meet him with timbrels and with dances. Apparently in times of victory, the custom was to greet the returning hero with dancing and rejoicing. Is it possible that we do not rejoice violently enough when God brings victory? This may be one reason why we do not see more victories wrought in the Church.

First Samuel 18 speaks of the return of David and Saul after the defeat of Goliath. Verses 6 and 7 tell us, "And it came to pass as they came, when David was returned from the slaughter of the Philistine, that the women came out of all cities of Israel, singing and dancing, to meet king Saul, with tabrets, with joy, and with instruments of musick. And the women answered one another as they played, and said, Saul hath slain his thousands, and David his ten thousands." Here, David was only a lad. He had not yet become the mighty warrior. As the spirit of prophecy rested upon the dancers, they sang concerning the victory of David, "David hath slain his ten thousands." It pays to take note of that which is prophesied in the midst of a high realm of anointing. First Samuel 21:10 and 11 and First Samuel 29:5 note that the people did pay attention to the word of the Lord which came while the people were dancing. It is necessary that we take heed to what God says through people who are abandoned to the anointing.

Song of Solomon 6:13 states, "Return, return, O Shulamite; return, return that we may look upon thee. What will ye see in the Shulamite? As it were the company of two armies." The word "company" has been translated from the Hebrew word that means "a dance." Apparently the Bride of Christ ascending into the presence of the King appears as a company of dancers. Could this be a prophetic picture of the Church which will be translated?

Several verses mention Abel-meholah, the "Meadow of the Dance." Abel-meholah was a place in Israel set aside for those who desired to dance and to rejoice during times of festivity. Abel-meholah is first mentioned in Judges 7:22 as one place to which the enemies of Israel were driven. Today the enemy still walks upon the meadow of the dance, for dancing is one of the most controversial forms of worship in the Church. Abel-meholah is again mentioned in First Kings 4:12, as one place from which the food for King Solomon was procured. The highest revelation of the Word of God is found where God's people are moving in liberty. Where God is moving, where the anointing is present, where joy and rejoicing are manifest, is where food will be found! Many who are critics of the present visitation and the liberty of worship for which it stands, still come from time to time to eat of the food produced at the meadow of the dance. From Abel-meholah they receive an abundant supply of food. First Kings 19:16 tells us that Elisha was born in Abel-meholah. Elisha speaks of the double portion ministry of the last-day Church. The Church born into the fulness of praise and worship, into the very high form of abandonment in the dance, is in line to receive the double portion of Elisha.

A Hebrew word meaning "a round dance" has been used in Psalms 30:11: "Thou has turned for me my mourning into dancing: thou hast put off my sackcloth, and girded me with gladness." Not only should we rejoice when things are looking good in the natural, but we should also rejoice when things look bleak and discouraging. God will cause us to rejoice and dance with joy even under the most adverse conditions. In times of mourning, God will put off our sackcloth and gird us with His gladness.

Psalms 149:3 states, "Let them praise his name in the dance." Here is an admonition that men worship God in the literal dance. Psalms 150:4 instructs God's people: "Praise him with the timbrel and dance." Because there was a musical instrument called the dantse, some people believe that Psalms 150 refers to a musical instrument rather than to the physical dance. Although this may be true, this fact does not detract from the truth of dancing. Since the timbrel was often associated with dancing, the phrase "praise him with the timbrel and dance" may be referring to the literal dance. In the mind of the psalmist, the playing of the timbrel and dancing may have been parallel.

Lamentation 5:15 states, "The joy of our heart is ceased; our *dance* is turned into mourning." One of the signs of a captive people is that dancing and rejoicing have ceased. However, God promised His people that He would not leave them in captivity. In Jeremiah 31:4, the Lord speaks to Israel, saying, "Again I will build thee, and thou shalt be built, O virgin of Israel: thou shalt again be adorned with thy tabrets, and shalt go forth in the *dances* of them that make merry." This verse has literally been fulfilled in natural Israel. On festive occasions, the people dance in the streets for the sheer joy of having their homeland restored to them. Today this verse is being fulfilled in spiritual Israel. The Church is experiencing times of festival as God's people rejoice in the knowledge that He has visited His people, and restoration is in progress. No wonder we dance today, for we have found our home!

Another promise of restoration is given in Jeremiah 31:12 and 13: "Therefore they shall come and sing in the height of Zion, and shall flow together to the goodness of the LORD, for wheat, and for wine, and for oil, and for the young of the flock and of the herd: and their soul shall be as a watered garden; and they shall not sorrow any more at all. Then shall the virgin rejoice in the *dance*, both young men and old together; for I will turn their mourning into joy, and will comfort them, and make them rejoice from their sorrow." There are three ingredients which must be in perfect balance in the last-day Church: the wheat, the wine, and the oil. First God must restore the wheat (the Word of God), for everything in the Body of Christ must be done on the basis of the revealed Word of God. Next, He must restore the wine, which is the joy of the Lord. Ephesians 5:18 states, "And be not drunk with wine, wherein is excess; but be filled with the Spirit." The oil speaks of anointing. A combination of the WORD, the JOY, and the ANOINTING restored to the Church, will produce unity in the Body. Jeremiah 31:13 tells us that when this takes place, THE VIRGIN SHALL REJOICE IN THE DANCE. The virgin is one who has been kept unspotted from the world. The experience of dancing before the Lord is reserved for men and women who have declared, "I will keep myself for God alone. I will have a single eye for His glory, so the river of God may flow through me in whatever manner He desires." One of the highest and holiest forms of worship the world will witness, will be that of God's people expressing in physical motion through vessels which have been cleansed and separated unto Him. Worshippers will dance before the Lord, for He has comforted them and made them to rejoice from their sorrow. It should be made absolutely clear, there is no place for sin or unholy living in this high realm of worship. The individual whose past is forgiven becomes, in that sense, a virgin but it is entirely necessary to walk in holiness and separation unto God.

A third Hebrew word that has been translated "dance" means "to dance (i.e., whirl)," and is found in Second Samuel 6:14: "And David *danced* before the LORD with all his might; and David was girded with a linen ephod." When the Ark of the Covenant was moved from the house of Obededom the Gittite to Jerusalem, David was filled with joy and began to dance with all his might, twisting and whirling before the presence of the Lord. First Chronicles 15:29 tells us that as he danced, he sprang about wildly, joyfully, jumping, leaping, and stamping. When David began to dance he removed every sign of his human position as leader of God's people, clothing himself with the garment of the priesthood. Michal, the daughter of Saul, despised David for this open display of joy. As a result, Michal became barren. When we observe God's people dancing before Him, one of two things will occur. To those who experience a longing for God and a desire to enter into the rejoicing will come liberty and joy; to those who choose to criticize God's people will come spiritual barrenness. Spiritual fruitfulness is dependent upon our *attitude* towards spiritual worship. Let this be a warning to God's people: despising the anointing can result in barrenness.

Today God is restoring His glory to the Church, and His people are laying aside every vestige of earthly glory and prestige. With complete abandonment and with great joy, they are dancing before the presence of His glory. God has not yet finished building His Temple. His purposes have not yet been accomplished in the earth. However, God's people are beginning to express great joy as they see the returning Ark of His Presence.

Another Hebrew word means "to stamp; i.e., to spring about wildly or for joy." This was used in First Chronicles 15:29, describing King David's dance of joy at the return of the Ark of the Covenant.

Ecclesiastes 3:1 and 4 states, "To every thing there is a season, and a time to every purpose under the heaven...A time to weep, and a time to laugh; a time to mourn, and a time to dance." From deep sorrow, God will bring forth great joy! From death, He will bring forth tremendous life! There is a time to mourn, and a time to spring about for joy!

Psalms 114:4 declares, "The mountains skipped like rams, and the little hills like lambs." Here the mountains skipped, or sprang about wildly at the presence of God. (I believe this literally took place at creation!) Why should not His people, who have experienced His redeeming grace, skip about also?

"Dance" has also been translated from a Hebrew word meaning "to twist or whirl (in a circular or spiral manner); i.e., to dance." This word is used in Judges 21:20 and 21, the account of how the children of Benjamin took wives for themselves. "Therefore they commanded the children of Benjamin, saying, Go and lie in wait in the vineyards; And see, and behold, if the daughters of Shiloh come out to dance in dances, then come ye out of the vineyards, and catch you every man his wife of the daughters of Shiloh, and go to the land of Benjamin." Verse 23 declares, "And the children of Benjamin did so, and took them wives, according to their number, of them that *danced*, whom they caught: and they went and returned unto their inheritance, and repaired the cities, and dwelt in them."

During this time of festival before the Lord, the young men waited in the vineyards to see the young women rejoice in God's presence. The men of Benjamin discovered a secret: when they needed wives, they went in search of spiritual women who danced in festival before Jehovah. Young men who select wives who are abandoned to the anointing, will have a solid foundation upon which their marriages can be built!

The circular form of this dance speaks of eternal unity. We are to be so at one with God our *lives* and our spirit will be a continual dance unto the Lord. This is a fulfilling of Romans 12:1, "I beseech you therefore, brethren, by the mercies of God, that ye present your bodies a living sacrifice, holy, acceptable unto God, which is your reasonable service." In "modern" dancing we find Satan's counterfeit for the true Godly dancing which is being restored to the Church. The dancing of the world is devilish, sensual and degrading; in the Church, dancing before the Lord is being birthed as a pure and holy form of worship.

In Scripture, the word "rejoice" has sometimes been translated from words which bear inference of leaping or springing about for joy. Some of the references which fall into this category will be discussed, for many of these references pertain to the dance.

In the Old Testament, the word "rejoice" has often been translated from a Hebrew word meaning "to spin around under the influence of any violent emotion; usually to rejoice, or (as cringing) fear." Psalms 2:11 states, "Serve the LORD with fear, and rejoice with trembling." God's people are to serve Him with fear and they are to rejoice. The Church that knows the fear of the Lord should literally rejoice in God and in His salvation. Psalms 9:14 declares, "That I may show forth all thy praise in the gates of the daughter of Zion: I will *rejoice* in thy salvation." David is saying that he will spin about with violent emotion and rejoice just because he has been redeemed. Psalms 13:5: "But I have trusted

in thy mercy; my heart shall *rejoice* in thy salvation."
Before our feet dance, our hearts must dance! Dancing
is an expression of the *condition of the heart.*

David said, "Make me to hear joy and gladness; that
the bones which thou hast broken may rejoice" (Ps.
51:8). David experienced a severe time of testing and
breaking before the Lord, but he recognized that
regardless of the circumstances in which he lived, his
relationship with the Lord brought to him joy and
rejoicing. David did not dance because someone
influenced his emotions by carnal or natural means; he
danced because he had received a fresh revelation of
the Almighty. With the testings and the pressures that
come into our lives today, we also must receive a fresh
revelation of God that we might leap, dance, and spin
about with joy in His presence.

Isaiah prophesied the word of the Lord, saying,
"Thou has multiplied the nation, and not increased the
joy: they joy before thee according to the joy in harvest,
and as men *rejoice* when they divide the spoil" (Isa.
9:3). There is a spiritual increase in our nation. There is
increase in church attendance, yet there is a great lack
of joy in Spirit filled churches. When God's people are
victorious over the work of the enemy, they experience
great joy; when men gather the harvest, gladness of
heart prevails. As God moves across our continent in
deliverance and restoration, men will jump for joy at
the ingathering of souls and the dividing of the spoil of
the enemy!

Many people who possess an abundance of material
goods, are not willing to enter into the simplicity of true
worship. They do not seem to want to rejoice in God.

However, Isaiah 29:19 declares, "The meek also shall increase their joy in the LORD, and the poor among men shall *rejoice* in the Holy One of Israel." The joy of the Lord is not contingent upon natural circumstances or possessions.

Other Scriptures containing this Hebrew word are: Psalms 16:9; Psalms 48:11; Psalms 97:1; Psalms 97:8; Psalms 118:24; Proverbs 23:24 and 25; Isaiah 61:10; Isaiah 65:18; Habakkuk 3:17 and 18; Zephaniah 3:14, Zechariah 9:9.

Three Hebrew words translated "rejoice" have similar meanings. These words mean "to jump (or leap) for joy; to exult." Psalms 68:4 exhorts, "Sing unto God, sing praises to his name: extol him that rideth upon the heavens by his name JAH, and *rejoice* before him." Psalms 5:11 states, "But let all those that put their trust in thee rejoice." Zephaniah 3:14 declares, "Sing, O daughter of Zion; shout, O Israel; be glad and *rejoice* with all the heart, O daughter of Jerusalem." These references instruct God's people to praise Him by singing, shouting, and rejoicing, by jumping and leaping for joy, and by exulting in Him. Jumping and leaping are not activities which should be excluded from a worship service, for God's people are told to rejoice *BEFORE HIM.* We are to jump and leap and exalt God in His very presence.

Other references containing these words which mean "to jump (or leap) for joy; to exult" are: First Samuel 2:1; Psalms 9:2; Psalms 108:7; Proverbs 11:10; Proverbs 23:16; Proverbs 28:12; Habakkuk 3:18.

Spiritual Dancing in the New Testament

In the New Testament the word "dance" has been translated from two words. One word means "to dance (from the rank-like or regular motion). The second word means "a ring or a round dance." Scriptures in which the word "dance" has been translated from the word "to dance" include Matthew 14:6 and Mark 6:22; the accounts of the daughter of Herodias dancing before Herod. Two other places in which this word is used are Matthew 11:17, and in Luke 7:32. "They are like unto children sitting in the marketplace, and calling one to another, and saying, We have piped unto you, and ye have not danced; we have mourned to you, and ye have not wept." Jesus is saying that nothing could please that generation. Today we should remember that when we pipe, there will always be those who will dance, and there will be those who will NOT. It is important that we seek to move in the anointing at all times!

Luke 15:11 through 32 presents the story of the prodigal son, a young man who left his father's house and wasted his inheritance with riotous living in a far country. When he returned to his father in repentance, his father had compassion upon him, clothed him, placed the ring of authority upon his finger, and prepared for him a feast. During this time of celebration, the elder brother who had been in the field returned to the house. He heard music and dancing (a ring or a round dance). When he was told the household was celebrating the return of his younger brother, he became angry and would not enter the house. The elder brother was bitter because his father had never prepared him a feast. He said, "Lo, these many years do I serve thee, neither transgressed I at any time thy commandment: and yet thou never gavest me a kid, that I might make merry with my friends: But as soon as this thy son was come, which hath devoured thy living with harlots, thou has killed for him the fatted calf." His father entreated him saying, "Son, thou art ever with me, and all that I have is thine. It was meet that we should make merry, and be glad: for this thy brother was dead, and is alive again; and was lost, and is found" (v. 29-32).

A similar situation exists in the Church today. Many who have squandered their inheritance have returned to Father's house and are rejoicing in their newly established relationship with Him. This rejoicing should not cause the elder brother to become bitter and cold, rather he should rejoice with those who have been restored, sharing their joy. There are people in the present move of God who realize the lateness of the hour, and how much time has been squandered. These people are pressing into the anointing with purpose and dedication far beyond that which they have ever experienced, for they are striving to enter into the fulness of relationship with their God. The restoration of these people should cause expressions of joy in the house of the Lord.

"Rejoice" has often been translated from a Greek word meaning "to jump for joy; to exult." Luke 1:46 and 47 relates the words of Mary, "My soul doth magnify the Lord, And my spirit hath *rejoiced* in God my Saviour." Before the feet of the worshipper begin to leap for joy, the spirit of the worshipper must leap. So great was Mary's joy at the thing which God had done, her spirit leaped for joy. Also the babe within Elisabeth's womb leaped for joy when she came into the presence of the unborn Christ (Luke 1:41). What leaping and rejoicing there will be when those who have been used to prepare the way of the Lord, witness the revelation of Christ within His Body!

John 8:56 states, "Your father Abraham *rejoiced* to see my day: and he saw it, and was glad." Abraham rejoiced in looking ahead to Jesus' day. How the spirit of that old patriarch must have leaped as God permitted him to see the days which were to come! No wonder he looked for a city with foundations, whose builder and maker is God (Heb. 11:10).

Acts 16:34 says that when the keeper of the prison brought Paul and Silas into his house, he set meat before them and *rejoiced*, believing in God with all his house. When Paul and Silas were in prison, they prayed and sang praises unto the Lord. Though their hands and feet were bound in stocks, these two praisers created the atmosphere for God to deliver. Not only were Paul and Silas delivered from prison, but the keeper of the prison was saved. The Bible tells us that after his salvation he leaped for joy, believing in God with all his house!

The spiritual dance that is being birthed in the Church today is more than expression of happiness because of natural circumstances; it is to be a response to persecution which will rise against the last-day Church. Matthew 5:11 and 12 states, "Blessed are ye, when men shall revile you, and persecute you, and shall say all manner of evil against you falsely, for my sake. Rejoice, and *be exceeding glad.*'' When persecution comes against God's people, they are to rejoice and jump for joy! If we who live in pleasant circumstances cannot rejoice before the Lord in times of worship, how will we be able to abandon ourselves to the rejoicing which must come in times of suffering? The spiritual dance is something the Church must experience in preparation for the last day.

First Peter 4:13 declares, "But *rejoice*, inasmuch as ye are partakers of Christ's sufferings; that, when his glory shall be revealed, ye may be glad also with exceeding joy.'' When we partake of Christ's suffering, we are to leap for joy. First Peter 1:6 and 7 states, "Wherein ye greatly *rejoice*, though now for a season, if need be, ye are in heaviness through manifold temptations: That the trial of your faith, being much more precious than of gold that perisheth, though it be tried with fire, might be found unto praise and honour and glory at the appearing of Jesus Christ.'' Although we may be in heaviness through many temptations, and our faith may be tried with fire, we are to rejoice and leap for joy. Even though we have not yet seen Him, we love Him, we believe in Him, and we rejoice with joy unspeakable and full of glory!

Revelation 19:7 announces, "Let us be glad and *rejoice*, and give honour to him: for the marriage of the Lamb is come, and his wife hath made herself ready.'' What a celebration of rejoicing there will be when the Lamb enters into union with His Bride! At that day we will rejoice and give honor unto Him!

Luke 10:20 and John 5:35 were also translated from this word meaning "to jump for joy; to exult."

Isaiah prophesied there would come a day when the lame man would leap as an hart (Isa. 35:6). This prophecy was literally fulfilled in Acts 3:6 through 8. Peter spoke to a man lame from his mother's womb, saying, "Silver and gold have I none; but such as I have give I thee: In the name of Jesus Christ of Nazareth rise up and walk." What a commotion this event must have caused when the beggar suddenly entered into the temple, walking and leaping and praising God!

A second account of a lame man leaping as an hart is presented in Acts 14:8 through 10. This man of Lystra, impotent in his feet, had been a cripple from his mother's womb. The Bible tells us, "The same heard Paul speak: who steadfastly beholding him, and perceiving that he had faith to be healed, Said with a loud voice, Stand upright on thy feet. And he leaped and walked." Again, we see a man who had been lame leaping for joy when he received strength in his feet.

Many people have wondered why those of us in this visitation are zealous and, at times, violent about our worship. They have not known that for years we sat daily at the gates of the temple watching ministers come and go, never having our personal needs met to the extent that we could enter in and become a part of what God was doing. For years we cried, "Oh, God, is this all there is for us?" In His mercy, God brought ministry who gave us more than we had asked for; we received strength where we thought we would never have strength. So overwhelming has been the work of God in our lives, that we do leap and shout and praise God!

Chapter Eight

God's Principle of Pouring Out

David was a worshipper. The book of Psalms presents songs of praise and worship which David sang unto God. What in David's life caused God to say, "I have found David the son of Jesse, a man after mine own heart"? (Acts 13:22).

The secret of success in David's life was not that he was a holy man. Although at the end of his life, David was a man who walked in holiness, righteousness, and purity, there were occasions when he was charged with unrighteousness. David lusted after a woman, caused her husband to be murdered, and did other things that exhibited the frailty of human nature. However, even in his human frailty, David was a man who discovered many divine principles, and as he found those principles and observed them, he became a man after God's heart. The secret of David's life was the fact that he was a man who deeply loved God, and each time he discovered one of God's principles, he immediately ordered his life accordingly.

Second Samuel 11 records the incident of David's sin with Bathsheba. When God spoke to David through Nathan the prophet, he immediately repented, saying, "I have sinned against the LORD" (2 Sam. 12:13). The principle of deep repentance is vital to our relationship with God. God will never free us from our problems until we repent of them. Regardless of how many times we discuss a problem, we will never be free of that problem until we have repented. God never smiled on David's sin, but because he found repentance in the presence of the Lord, God forgave his sin.

Another example of David walking in the principles of God is found in 1 Samuel 24:1 through 7. Saul went into a cave, and David and his men remained in the sides of the cave. David's men tempted him, saying, "Behold the day of which the Lord said unto thee, Behold, I will deliver thine enemy into thine hand, that thou mayest do to him as it shall seem good unto thee," (v.4). He cut off the skirt of Saul's garment. The Bible tells us that David was convicted because he cut off Saul's skirt. He said, "The LORD forbid that I should do this thing unto my master, the LORD's anointed, to stretch forth mine hand against him, seeing he is the anointed of the LORD" (v.6). Here David discovered God's principle of forgiveness, and it became revelation in his life. He saw that he was not to take vengeance upon his enemy, but to forgive even as God forgives. Throughout the Psalms David wrote much about forgiveness, because he had a meeting with the God of forgiveness.

Again, an example of David walking in the principles of God is found in 2 Samuel 23:13 through 17. The account of David thirsting for water from the well of Bethlehem, presents the principle of pouring out as one of the best examples of worship in the Word of God.

"And three of the thirty chief went down, and came to David in the harvest time unto the cave of Adullam: and the troop of the Philistines pitched in the valley of Rephaim. And David was then in an hold, and the garrison of the Philistines was then in Bethlehem. And David longed, and said, Oh that one would give me drink of the water of the well of Bethlehem, which is by the gate! And the three mighty men brake through the host of the Philistines, and drew water out of the well of Bethlehem, that was by the gate, and took it, and brought it to David: nevertheless he would not drink thereof, BUT POURED IT OUT UNTO THE LORD. And he said, Be it far from me, O LORD, that I should do this: is not this the blood of the men that went in jeopardy of their lives? therefore he would not drink it. These things did these three mighty men."

At the time of harvest, David was in the cave of Adullam. He longed for a drink of water from the well of Bethlehem, which is by the gate. The water from the well of Bethlehem was very delicious. Possibly this water was sweeter, fresher, and contained less alkaline and minerals, than did the water near the cave of Adullam. Indeed, there was a longing in David's heart for a drink of the water which would satisfy him more deeply than anything else at that time.

David was thirsty for some of that refreshing water, but between him and the thing he desired was the host of the Philistines. Three mighty men broke through the host of the Philistines, drew water from the well of

Bethlehem, and brought the water to David. They risked their own lives in order that David might have a drink of water from that well. When David received the water, he did not drink it, but poured it out unto the Lord, saying, "Is not this the blood of the men that went in jeopardy of their lives?"

David had every right to drink of that water. The drink from the well of Bethlehem, that thing for which his soul had longed, was his to do with as he pleased. But when he realized the cost with which that water had been purchased, it turned to blood in his hands. At that moment, it seemed as though the Spirit of God lifted David into a higher dimension, and he began to touch a principle of God. David had a legal right to drink that water, but when he received it, he realized there was a higher principle than drinking it and satisfying himself. David took the water he had asked for, water which had been brought to him for the purpose of satisfying him and fulfilling his desire, and poured it out on the ground as an offering unto the Lord.

Often I have wondered what those three mighty men thought as they watched David take the water for which they had risked their lives, and pour it upon the ground. In the natural, these men could have been disgusted with David. They might have thought they had risked their lives in vain. The disciples had this same attitude toward the woman who broke an alabaster box of ointment upon Jesus (Matt.26:8). They said, "That is a waste! If she wanted to throw it away, she had no business doing it that way. She should have sold it and given the proceeds to the poor." Jesus answered them, "Why trouble ye the woman? for she hath wrought a good work upon me...Verily I say unto you, Wheresoever this gospel shall be preached in the whole world, there shall also this, that this woman hath done, be told for a memorial of her" (Matt. 26:10-13). The disciples called the pouring out a waste, but Jesus said that forever it would be a memorial of her. He knew it would have been a waste if it had NOT been poured out!

We are a needy people who require fulfillment and satisfaction. There is a tendency for us to complain, saying, "The Lord did not bless me tonight. The service was not good." Our purpose in coming to the house of the Lord should not be for blessing, but for pouring out. We come to the house of the Lord that we might take everything He has given to us, and pour it back in worship unto Him. When we touch that principle of pouring out everything at His feet, then no longer do we relate to God from a horizontal level of praise, but we worship Him through the vertical level of relationship that we might please HIS heart.

It is time we realized that God is tired of "give me." "Give me a new car, a better house, a large paycheck, new clothes, a different church," and the list never ends. It is time we stopped demanding things from God! We need to come before Him and say, "Lord, You have been so wonderful to me. You have saved me, baptized me, and filled me with Your Holy Spirit. I am a child of the King and I bear Your Name proudly. It does not matter if I live in a tent or if I drive a Model T, Lord, You have been wonderful to me." When we begin to pour out unto the Lord everything He has given us, we touch a higher dimension in God than always saying, "God is a good God, and He will give us everything we want."

You cannot be a worshipper until you realize what it is to give up your rights. You cannot become a worshipper until the deepest desires of your heart have been poured out in worship unto the Lord. I know what it is to burn for the mission field and the nations of the earth. I know what it is to see missionaries off at the airport, doing what I would give my life to do. There is a higher dimension in God than going to the foreign fields; that of saying, "God, whether I go or I stay is not important, even though You told me that I would go. You said I would be a missionary, a singer, or a pastor, I just want to take your promise *to me*, and pour it out upon the ground as an offering unto You. I want to die to every right I have, in order that I might become a worshipper." David was a mighty man of valour, he and his army defeated the Philistines. David reigned king over Israel, and he saw the realization of the everlasting covenant God had made with him. Before he saw any of these things come to pass, David had to touch the principle of pouring out, so that everything within him would be poured out in worship unto his God. David found out that a desire is never really satisfied until it has been given unto the Lord, and has been poured out in worship at His feet. That does not involve running around saying, "I do not care anymore." You will care more than you ever cared in all your life. However, when you touch this principle of worship, your desire is poured out unto Him, and it does not really matter as long as He receives the glory.

One person who had experienced this type of relationship said to me, "You know, when I really touched worship, suddenly everything else became of little importance!" Indeed, at the moment when David poured out the water from Bethlehem's well, I do not think he even considered the Philistines. To him there was not a Philistine in existence; there existed only David and God. If we desire to become worshippers, God will bring to us those times in His presence when there are no Philistines. We will come alone into the presence of God, pouring out everything we have as an offering unto Him. God will accept that offering; new life will spring from earth that once was barren, because our lives were poured out unto Him in worship.

Pouring Out at the Feet of Jesus

Luke 7:36 through 50 tells of a woman who was delivered from a life of sin through the ministry of Jesus. When the woman met Jesus, He ministered to her, forgave her, and cleansed her, then she saw herself not as a woman of the streets, but as a virgin clean and pure. When she discovered that Jesus was in the house of Simon the Pharisee, she went to the house, taking with her an alabaster box of ointment. It was obvious that this woman had previously had an encounter with Jesus; this is indicated by the fact that she purposely took with her the alabaster box of costly ointment. She was deeply touched because Jesus had delivered her, and when she came into His presence she began to weep. As she remembered the life that she had lived, she poured out her tears upon His feet.

The bottle of tears, which every member of a family

possessed, usually was a slender bottle with a broad base and a funnel-shaped top. When a person cried, the tears were brushed into the bottle. The bottle of tears was a very precious possession, for the tears represented the intimate personal feelings and experiences of its owner. I believe the woman who came to Jesus had her bottle of tears, and she poured them upon His feet, adding to them all of her present tears. Everything life had held for her, she poured out at the feet of Jesus. Then she wiped His feet with the hairs of her head, kissed His feet, and anointed them with the costly ointment contained in the alabaster box.

The Bible tells us that God bottles up the tears of His saints. Psalms 56:8 declares, "Thou tellest my wanderings: put thou my tears into thy bottle." Our tears shed in times of joy, sorrow, tragedy, heartache, anger, frustration, disappointment, and happiness have been preserved by the Lord. In times of worship we can take our bottle of tears and pour them out at the feet of Jesus. Many of us do not realize the tremendous thing God has done for us in redemption. He has purchased us, forgiven, and cleansed us. We stand in His presence as virgins, clean and pure; fully restored. The most important thing we can do is pour out our lives in His presence.

Many people have said to me, "When I was young, I was called to the ministry, but I blew it. There is no way I can ever go into the ministry now." With great joy I am able to say to these people, "The Bible says that God will give back the wasted years, the years that the locust and the cankerworm have eaten (Joel 2:25). God will restore your life, but first you must pour out your desires at His feet.'' While some people constantly live in a realm of praise, others take all of the experiences that life has brought and pour them out in the worship unto the Lord. These are the people whom God restores. These are the people whom God picks up, and says, "You are restored. Go your way.'' These are the people to whom God is giving the desire of their hearts because they touched the principle of pouring out. Many times I have wondered what grew up out of the desert land where David poured the water from the well of Bethlehem, for water poured out upon earth becomes a source of life to the barren land. There is no telling what will spring up from your barren earth once you take everything life has held for you, and pour it out as an act of worship. You can watch the most negative things in your life being transformed into a source of joy as you pour out those experiences at His feet.

There are some people who harbor bitter memories so painful that they can neither talk, nor think objectively about them. Constantly, they are haunted by shadows of the past. Even though they do the appropriate things and seem to receive the external blessings of God, something is blocking them from becoming true worshippers. There is a place in God where these memories can be healed, and these lives made whole. In this realm of healing, praise is not the answer. The answer is a relationship with Jesus in which the person might pour out these memories.

Think of the memories that woman must have had when she poured out those tears at His feet. She had suffered abuse at the hands of cruel men, then found a

Man who did not want to abuse her! She who suffered humiliation and shame, now found One Who had the power of God to restore to her life and human dignity. Along with the tears, she poured out at His feet all the bitter experiences that life had held for her. When she arose, it was as though these experiences never happened, because they were poured out in worship unto the Lord.

Abraham and Isaac

Genesis 22 presents the account of Abraham and Isaac. The Bible tells us that the Lord tempted (or tested) Abraham, telling him to take Isaac into the land of Moriah and offer him there for a burnt offering. Abraham rose early in the morning and set out for Moriah, taking with him Isaac, two young men, and wood for the burnt offering. "Then on the third day Abraham lifted up his eyes, and saw the place afar off" (v.4). Many of us are standing where Abraham stood on the morning of that third day, seeing the place afar off. We do not know all that the third day involves, but we know we must follow the command of the Lord.

I am convinced that the Church is standing spiritually where Abraham stood on that morning when he saw the place "afar off." I am sure he did not have the slightest idea what God had in store for him, nor did he know the eternal implications involved in his complete obedience to the command of God. As Abraham viewed the land, he knew that whatever lay ahead, he had no choice, HE MUST FOLLOW!

While some people are very content to live for today, never lifting their eyes to behold the day which is just ahead, there are those among God's people who carry a very great sense of destiny. Knowing by the Spirit that God is about to birth a new day, they view the land afar off. I am not sure I understand all that is involved in God's future for the Church, and the eternal implications of that day, but there is a consuming vision which lives and grows within me. GOD IS BIRTHING A NEW DAY IN THE CHURCH! The new day will surely involve the laying down of many an "Isaac" and many of our God-given "rights." This may include the right to ministry, and perhaps our own ideas of Church order, that His divine order might be revealed. In contrast with the complete joy of coming into the fulness of relationship with Him, the sacrifice is of no consequence. Some men live for time, but *WORSHIPPERS LIVE FOR ETERNITY!*

I believe Abraham walked with God in such a way that when God said, "Take now your son Isaac, whom you love very much, and give him for a burnt offering to Me," Abraham immediately declared, "Lord, I will offer Isaac to You as an act of worship." We too, can respond saying, "Lord, this is not really a sacrifice, but an act of worship. Because I love you much more than I love this offering, it is a pleasure to pour it out before You." God is pleased when we offer this kind of sacrifice to Him. Many times the thing we pour out to God in worship, God will return to us.

So great was Abraham's confidence in God, even though he knew the worship involved the sacrifice of Isaac, he said to the young men who accompanied them, "Abide ye here with the ass; and *I AND THE LAD WILL* go yonder and worship and *COME AGAIN* to you" (v.5). Although Abraham was going to sacrifice his only son, he believed "God, who quickeneth the dead, and calleth those things which be not as though they were" (Rom. 4:17). When Abraham stretched forth his hand to slay Isaac, the angel of the Lord called to him and said, "Lay not thine hand upon the lad, neither do thou anything unto him: for now I know that thou fearest God, seeing thou hast not withheld thy son, thine only son, from me" (Gen. 22:12). As Abraham lifted up his eyes, he saw a ram caught in a thicket by his horns. Instead of his son, Abraham offered up the ram for a burnt offering. *ABRAHAM HAD MET THE GOD OF RESURRECTION* (Heb. 11:17-19).

As parents, there is nothing we desire more than to see our children serve God with all their hearts, even outrunning us in spiritual things. We can train our children in the ways of God, we can pray for them and do everything we know to do for them, but there comes a time when we must offer our children unto the Lord. We must pour them out unto God, saying, "Lord, I want to offer my children unto You as an act of worship. Whether they walk in God or whether they do not, I am offering them unto You." When we offer our children unto the Lord, "God, who quickeneth the dead, and calleth those things which be not as though they were" will touch their lives with His resurrection power and they will never be the same!

Genesis 22:15 tells us that the angel of the Lord called to Abraham a second time, saying, "By myself have I sworn, saith the LORD, for because thou hast done this thing, and hast not withheld thy son, thine only son: That in blessing I will bless thee, and in multiplying I will multiply thy seed as the stars of the heaven, and as the sand which is upon the sea shore; and thy seed shall possess the gate of his enemies; And in thy seed shall all the nations of the earth be blessed; because thou hast obeyed my voice" (v. 16-18). Here we see the results of Abraham's obedience to the Word of the Lord. God said that He would bless Abraham and multiply his seed. In addition, Abraham's seed would possess the gate of his enemies. God is never satisfied when His people are in bondage. He will see that the authority of the enemy is torn down. Finally, God said that in Abraham's seed would ALL the nations of the earth be blessed. We are to put our offerings upon our Mount Moriah. Only that which is offered in death will spring forth in resurrection life. Only from that which has been offered to God will we receive blessing. When our offerings have been poured out, THEN all the nations of the earth will be blessed. The Church that reaches the nations of the earth for Christ, will be the Church which has poured out everything as an offering upon the mountain of worship. From that lonely mountain, will spring forth life which will touch the nations.

The Father and The Eternal Son

John 3:16 states, "For God so loved the world, that he gave his only begotten Son, that whosoever believeth in him should not perish, but have everlasting life." Jesus, the Son of God, was the object of the Father's pouring out long before the creation of the world. Although Calvary demonstrated the eternal principle of pouring out, it was not the birthplace of the cross principle, for the Word tells us that Jesus was "the

Lamb slain from the foundation of the world" (Rev. 13:8). Somewhere in eternity the Father poured out the Son. Just as Isaac was offered on Mount Moriah, so Jesus was offered upon Mount Calvary. Jesus was broken just as the alabaster box was broken. Jesus was poured out into the earth in the same manner the water from the well of Bethlehem was poured out. Today we see the life which sprang from the earth, the Church of the Lord Jesus Christ.

Philippians 2:5 states, "Let this mind be in you, which was also in Christ Jesus." We are to have the same attitude or point of view toward pouring out as did Jesus, when He said in Hebrews 10:7, "Then said I, Lo, I come (in the volume of the book it is written of me,) to do thy will, O God." Jesus desired to do the will of the Father, and He was willing to be poured out.

What was involved in that pouring out of Jesus? Philippians 2:6 through 8 says of Jesus, "Who, being in the form of God, thought it not robbery to be equal with God: But made himself of no reputation, and took upon him the form of a servant, and was made in the likeness of men: And being found in fashion as a man, he humbled himself, and became obedient unto death, even the death of the cross." John 1:14 tells us, "The Word was made flesh, and dwelt among us." Hebrews 2:14 through 16 says that Jesus became partaker of flesh and blood, taking on Him the seed of Abraham. When Jesus made Himself of no reputation, He poured out His divine nature and took upon Himself the nature of man. He Who is the Son of God, Who is the very nature of God, submitted Himself to the will of His Father, by taking upon Himself human nature, and becoming obedient unto death. He literally laid aside His glory. He laid aside His sonship. He laid aside His kingship. Hebrews 12:2 tells us that Jesus, "who for the joy that was set before him endured the cross, despising the shame." Jesus knew no resistance to the Father's will. Just as Isaac bore the wood up Mount Moriah, so Jesus bore the cross to Calvary. Jesus became God's Isaac, the One Who was sacrificed that life might flow into the earth.

There is a realm in God where we say, "I will not only pour out unto the Lord, but I am ready to be poured out." John 12:24 states, "Except a corn of wheat fall into the ground and die, it abideth alone: but if it die, it bringeth forth much fruit." In the natural, man would think that the water poured out by David onto the earth was wasted. However, in the heart of David, God saw the principle of pouring out in worship. A person who possesses wheat has two alternatives: He may grind the wheat into flour and make it into bread to feed the hungry, who will only become hungry again, or he can plant the wheat in the ground that it might die, and multiply to bring forth life to feed a multitude. If we choose to grind the wheat into flour nobody has the right to criticize us, for one purpose of wheat is that it might be made into flour. But if we see the higher principle, and sow the wheat into the earth, much fruit will be brought forth. God chose to sow His Son into the earth. From Mount Calvary was produced much fruit, and from that ultimate of pouring out, there was created a glorious Church, without spot or wrinkle or any such thing.

Philippians 2:9 through 11 states, "Wherefore God

also hath highly exalted him, and given him a name which is above every name: That at the name of Jesus every knee should bow...And that every tongue should confess that Jesus Christ is Lord, to the glory of God the Father." Because Jesus was obedient to the death of the cross, and He became the corn of wheat which fell into the ground and died, He became the firstfruits among many brethren.

Every ministry which God has put into the Church must become obedient unto death. God is not interested in big-time ministries, neither does God want an Ishmael in what He is doing today. God wants an Isaac that will be poured out. God wants the principle of pouring out working in our lives to the extent that not only will we be willing *to pour out our greatest desire,* but also be willing *to be poured out.* If Jesus had said to the Father, "Father, I love You too much to leave You," we would still be lost in sin. Jesus was not only willing to become the Saviour of the world, He also was willing to be poured out, that the heart of the Father might be satisfied. Jesus, the object of that eternal principle of pouring out, knew that God was pouring Him into the earth. He knew if He would become the corn of wheat that was poured into the ground to die, resurrection life would spring forth. He Who was willing to be poured out, is now multiplied in the nations of the earth.

Because God was willing to pour out His Son and because the Son was willing to be poured out, we have a precedent for any act of pouring out which God might ask of us. We can pour out ministry, friends, possessions, and the desires of our hearts. We, ourselves, can be poured out. We can give up our legal and legitimate rights to possessions, ministry, friendships, and any other rights which we might have, and become that corn of wheat which falls into the ground and dies, that much fruit might be brought forth.

Bibliography

EXPOSITOR'S GREEK NEW TESTAMENT. W.R. Nicoll, ed., W.B. Eerdman's, Grand Rapids, Mich., 1951. Used by permission.

THE AMPLIFIED BIBLE, Old Testament. Copyright 1962, 1964 by Zondervan Publishing House. Used by permission.

THE NEW ENGLISH BIBLE. Copyright The delegates of Oxford University Press and the Syndics of the Cambridge University Press 1961, 1970. Reprinted by permission.

B. M. Bowen, STRANGE SCRIPTURES THAT PERPLEX THE WESTERN MIND. W. B. Eerdman's, Grand Rapids, Mich., 1972.

UNGER'S BIBLE DICTIONARY by Merrill F. Unger. Copyright 1957, 1961, 1966. Moody Press, Moody Bible Institute of Chicago, p. 237. Used by permission.

Notes